I Leap for Joy

by
Sister Mary Bernard

edited by
Howard Earl

LOGOS INTERNATIONAL
PLAINFIELD, NEW JERSEY

Unless otherwise identified, all Scriptures are from
The New American Bible, © 1970, by the Catholic Press.

Abbreviations for other versions of the Bible:
  KJV = King James' version
  TAB = The Amplified Bible, © 1965 by Zondervan
      Publishing House.

to the
Blessed Trinity
who
brought me
into the fullness and joy
of
Christianity

Let this same attitude and purpose and humble mind be in you which was in Christ Jesus.—Let Him be your example humility. (Phil. 2:5 TAB)

Though He was in the form of God,
   he did not deem equality with God
   something to be grasped at.
Rather, he emptied himself
   and took the form of a slave,
   being born in the likeness of men.
He was known to be of human estate,
   and it was thus that he humbled
      himself,
   obediently accepting even death,
   death on a cross!
   God highly exalted him
   and bestowed on him the name
   above every other name,
So that at Jesus' name
   every knee must bend
   in the heavens, on the earth,
   and under the earth,
   and every tongue proclaim
   to the glory of God the Father:
JESUS CHRIST IS LORD!
               (Phil. 2:6-11)

Contents

Preface

During my life, I have met many people searching in vain for joy, peace, and happiness. Burdened with fears and complaints, they have asked, "Why has God treated me in this way?" Confronted with the suggestion that perhaps they themselves were responsible for their predicament, they have thrown up their hands and said, "Well, then, what can we do about it?"

Scientists have intimated that technology could solve all our problems. Educators have said that academic training is the answer, that college degrees and good jobs would bring happiness. But materialism has only accentuated the void of unfulfilled lives.

I can identify with the searchers, because in my own early childhood, I, too, had an empty heart. But now my heart is full—I have found the answer to my search.

What I have found, all can find—the love, joy, and peace of saying yes to God and living in an intimate, personal relationship with the Jesus who invites us, "If any man thirst, let him come unto me, and drink" (John 7:37 KJV).

This book is written to explain how I came to drink from the well of living water—the well that never runs dry, the well that offers life eternal.

What we have seen and heard, we proclaim in turn to you so that you may share life with us. This fellowship of ours is with the Father and with His Son, Jesus Christ. Indeed, our purpose in writing this to you, is that our joy may be complete. (I John 1:3-4)

Chapter 1
Faith and Patience

I first saw Joe when his mother brought him into the living room in a wheelchair. His large head was covered with an abundance of dark brown, curly hair. His legs hung from the chair limp and useless, emaciated by muscular dystrophy of the most common type. The disease is characterized by the pseudohypertrophy of muscles, especially those of the calves of the legs, and gradually lessens the ability of the child to walk until by the time he reaches his teens, he has completely lost the use of his legs. Seldom do victims of this type of muscular dystrophy live to adult life.

Joe could neither read, write, nor memorize. Fully convinced he had only a short time to live, he showed no interest in pursuing an education. Instead, he spent most of his waking hours before the television set.

There had been other teachers before me who had volunteered to give Joe religious instruction in his home, but none had returned after the first visit because of Joe's resentment toward them and education in general. He did not want to be bothered with Roman Catholic Sisters when he could watch television.

I determined to win his friendship.

It was not easy, but as I returned week after week to give Joe his instruction, I began to detect a change in him. He seemed puzzled as I took his rebuffs without any unkind replies, as I reached out to him with love and told him about the love of Jesus Christ for him. There came a time when his dark eyes danced with excitement as he was wheeled into the living room and saw me waiting. He had found two who cared for him —Jesus and me.

Slowly he began to understand that the Creator had made him for Himself. Despite the ungratefulness of man, God had sent His Son into the world to redeem man, to give what no one else could give—love in the present and eternal happiness in heaven.

After a time, it was decided that Joe and I should vacate the living room so that Joe's younger brother, now also confined to a wheelchair by muscular dystrophy, might take his instruction there. Joe and I continued our lessons in his bedroom. There was another change, too, a change in Joe's attitude toward me. He began to confide in me as a trusted friend.

One day he very timidly disclosed that he had a hobby.

"What is it, Joe?" I asked.

"Drawing horses. Would you like to see one, Sister Mary?"

"Would I!" Horses, and especially ponies, had always held an attraction for me even as a little tyke.

I told Joe that when I was a little girl, one day I saw a sign on a vacant lot: "Pony Rides, 25¢." I didn't have a quarter, so I rushed home to get one from my mother. But she was not at home, and for a moment, I was crushed. Then I remembered the tall pitcher in the dining room where my mother kept her change. It didn't take long to fish out three quarters, and in no time, I was waiting in line with other children for my pony rides —three of them! On my third time around, the pony stopped to graze on some luscious green grass. When he lowered his head to the ground, I gleefully slid down his long neck into the grass.

Afterward, I rushed home to tell mother about the grand time I had riding the pony. But before I could say a word, I suddenly realized that I had taken money that didn't belong to me. Immediately, I was on my knees sobbing.

"What's wrong, Mary?" mother asked.

As I continued to sob, she took me on her lap and held me close. Finally, between sobs, I blurted out what I had done. Tenderly, my mother made me understand that I had already paid the penalty for my misdeed, but that it should be a lesson to keep me from ever again taking anything that did not belong to me.

Joe listened patiently to my story, and when I finished, he asked, "Did you?"

"Did I what?"

"Ever take anything after that that didn't belong to you?"

"No, not that I remember, Joe. Now, let's look at your drawings."

From beside him in the wheelchair, he brought forth a drawing of a horse. "This is one," he said softly, almost apologetically.

"Who taught you to draw so beautifully?"

"No one, Sister Mary. I learned by myself.

The sketch was little short of a masterpiece, and I told him so. From then on, after nearly every visit, I left with one of Joe's drawings.

Our friendship strengthened, and so did Joe's love for Jesus Christ. His desire to know more about the Savior increased daily. Happy with this development, I brought many visual aids to teach Joe the basics of Christianity. Showing him God's love, I tried to encourage him to develop patience, confidence, perseverance, and above all, to grow in prayer and the love of God.

Joe's natural virtues did develop. He became kinder to his younger brothers and sisters, and respectful and grateful to his parents. He began to grow spiritually, too. Soon I could see him beginning to accept his physical condition without resentment. "Jesus suffered so much for me," he said one day, "I can afford to suffer a little for Him." Then he accepted Jesus as his Lord and Savior, acknowledging Jesus' great love for him.

One day, not long after that, Joe surprised me by asking, "When you come back to this life after death, what kind of an animal would you like to be?" His eyes and entire manner denoted excited expectation as he awaited my reply.

"Where did you get that idea?" I asked him.

He told me that he had watched a television comedy program in which reincarnation was shown as a reality. To Joe, it was more than mere entertainment. It threatened what I had taught him about his life after death with Christ.

I explained to Joe the impossibility of reincarnation. Going back over previous lessons, I reminded Joe that God made animals to be under the dominion of man.

"Were you made to become a beast, or were you made for some higher purpose?" I asked.

Joe thought for a moment, then replied, "I was made to love and glorify God. I was made in God's image. I can't change that, can I, Sister Mary?"

"No, you cannot," I replied.

Joe sighed heavily, and with that deep breath, I knew his security in God was intact. "God loves you more than all the sparrows and animals in the world," I explained. "You are going to be a part forever of the beauty, peace, and contentment of heaven, free from sickness, suffering, and pain."

After our little discussion, Joe came alive with a new joy in his heart and a new understanding of why Jesus had come into the world.

"I really belong to Jesus now," he told me one day with such confidence that there was no room for doubt.

"Yes," I answered. "And you are going to receive Holy Communion right here tomorrow, Joe, and from then on, on the first Friday of every month."

His eyes reflected the joy my promise brought to him.

That was the last time I saw Joe in his wheelchair. He had a cold the following week, and I made my stay short, feeding him his lunch and instructing him as he lay in bed. How much he had changed since the first time I had seen him! His face was pale and gaunt, but his eyes mirrored love and happiness.

Joe knew that his life was ebbing away. He longed to be with Jesus as night after night he gazed upon a luminous cross I had given him.

As Joe grew visibly weaker, I asked the parish priest to visit him, but there was some misunderstanding, and the priest failed to go. I suggested to his mother that Joe would appreciate nightly prayers with the family gathered around his bed. This, too, was put off.

Then one night, Joe himself took charge. He asked the family to kneel around his bed for their prayers, and they did.

The next morning, Joe's mother walked into the bedroom. "I have to go on an errand," she said. "I'll be back very soon. Your sister is here if you need anything."

"That's all right," Joe answered. "I'm not afraid anymore. Jesus is with me."

She brushed his cheek with her lips and left the room. When she returned, Joe was with Jesus. His wasted body lay on the bed, his eyes focused on the cross on the wall.

Chapter 2
God's Leading

My first experience with physical pain came when I was a child. One day, while riding my bicycle, I fell on the railroad tracks and cut my knee. Mother didn't seem to consider it a serious injury as she bandaged it, but some days later, my knee began to hurt. As the days passed, the pain increased, and severe soreness extended up and down the leg. Mother applied hot packs, hoping to draw the poison to a head, but the pain became so excruciating that dad called the doctor in the middle of the night.

"Bad! Very bad!" the doctor said, shaking his head disapprovingly. "Blood poisoning. You should have called me sooner. The girl may lose her leg."

He performed surgery on my knee that night as I lay in bed. For weeks, I visited his office daily, and he inserted cotton swabs soaked in iodine to cleanse the wound and aid the healing process. Eventually, the poison left the leg, and the wound healed, but I was not permitted to ride my bicycle again.

I was a normal child with the usual liking for play. Once my mother sent me to the butcher shop for some pork chops. On the way home, I stopped to swing for a while on the park playground, placing the package of chops on the ground nearby. Soon I was sailing back and forth through the air, held in space by two strands of rope and a narrow board seat.

It was such a lovely day, and

swooshing through the air was so delightful, that I lost track of time. When mother came looking for me, she discovered me enjoying life with no thought about the errand on which she had sent me. We found the paper in which the meat had been wrapped, and a short distance away, two dogs were licking their chops.

One Sunday morning, I made a rather crucial decision in my young life. I decided I would not go to Mass. It was perfectly all right, I reasoned, for my two sisters to attend Mass each Sunday, but why should I have to go when our parents never attended?

"Why should I go to church when you don't?" I asked my dad. His reply was simple, leaving no doubt as to his convictions.

"It's not what I do, Mary," he said. "It's what I consider best for you. I want you to go to church every Sunday because it will give you the moral strength, supplied by God, to face the problems of life in your future years."

Later, I felt a great longing to know more about Jesus, and I used to visit the public library and look at the holy books and pictures of Jesus I found there. While I was receiving instructions for my first Holy Communion, the curate gave me an insight into the personal love of Jesus. My Savior became so real to me that I learned to talk to Him in prayer. I loved Him and knew He loved me. Jesus became my best friend.

When I was in the eighth grade, dad and mother separated, and a year after that, mother went to be with the Lord.

A few days after her funeral, a friend of the family came to keep us company for a week. We had many material possessions, including a fine collection of cut glass, and our guest raved continuously about the many fine things in our home. Her eyes and heart were filled with envy, while my heart was filled with a void. With a child's intuition, I sensed that someone besides my mother was missing— Jesus Christ had never been the head of our home.

Although my sisters and I continued to attend church every Sunday, we were still hungry for the spiritual food that alone can satisfy the heart.

One Sunday we were running late, and I stepped on the accelerator rather heavily. Suddenly a siren sounded, and a patrol car came up alongside us. I pulled over to the side of the road and stopped.

"Where do you think you're going?" the officer barked at me as he approached the car.

"We're hurrying to get to church," I replied.

He poked his head through the open window and gazed into the back seat. "Come on now," he said in a booming voice. "Where've you got the boys stashed away?"

I smiled, assured him no boys were involved, and once again emphasized that we were hurrying to church. He looked rather quizzically at the three of us and demanded, "Let's see your driver's license!"

I dug into my purse and came up with the special driver's license I had obtained when I was only fourteen. The officer looked at it for a suspenseful minute, then returned it with a smile. "All right, kids," he said. "Be on your way—but use a lighter foot on that accelerator."

My first year in high school, I followed my peers, even taking a try at cigarettes, but nothing seemed to satisfy me until somehow I came up with the idea that I should try to be of service to others. I had a longing to teach retarded children, and spent hours in the public library poring over books on psychology and methods of teaching "special" children.

Although I didn't realize it at the time, the Lord was already preparing me for my future vocation.

Six months after mother's death, our family home was sold, and my sisters—Joan and Evelyn—and I moved to San Francisco to be near my godparents. When Evelyn's health became a matter of concern, the doctor suggested that she leave the Bay area. Joan and I accompanied her to Hollywood.

In Hollywood, I tried to obtain engagements as a classical ballet dancer. Before her marriage, my mother had been a dancer in the Ziegfeld Follies on Broadway, and she had started me on a dancing career early. When I was only six years old, I had performed in local theaters, and received the huge sum of one dollar and fifty cents for each performance. In addition, our whole family got to stay and see a movie — free!

Because I was double-jointed, I was able to perform acrobatic dancing feats beyond the capabilities of a normal individual. A special feature of my dance number was to stand flat-footed on one foot and raise the other foot over my head, resting the sole of that foot on my chest. This physical abnormality propelled me to youthful stardom, but it was to cause me a severe physical problem later in life.

For nearly eight years, I had bathed in the dazzling glare of publicity, performing my various steps to beautiful music while enveloped in the soft glow of colored lights. But now, Hollywood had no place for me.

Meanwhile, Evelyn regained her health, and we went to Oakland where we renewed our contacts with dad after two years of practically no communication between us.

I had been a high school dropout, filling in with a course at a design and dressmaking school in San Francisco. While in Hollywood, I had concluded that a high school diploma would be a good thing to have, and I decided to continue my education at Alameda High. The only place dad could find for me to live in Alameda was a room in the home of a widow who lived near our old neighborhood. I rebelled at the thought of returning to the place of painful memories, but I seemed to understand, perhaps through dad's persuasion, that this was where God wanted me.

The Cardinet family, famous for their U NO candy bars, lived across the street from me. Their daughter Lorraine was a new convert to Catholicism. She introduced me to the Sisters who were teaching in our parish. This was my first acquaintance with Catholic Sisters, even though I had been a Catholic all my life.

During the Thanksgiving holiday, the Sisters invited Lorraine and me to attend a retreat at the Catholic Girls Conference in Oakland. I wanted to go, but had some fears about Sisters because I had never really known any.

"Aw, come on, Mary," Lorraine pleaded.

"I'll go," I finally promised her, "provided we are allowed to enjoy ourselves and don't have to become too friendly with the Sisters. I don't want any of them flitting about me, raving about how wonderful it is to be a Sister."

"I can't make any promises for the Sisters," Lorraine said, "but if you find anything you don't like and want to leave the retreat, I will leave with you."

The very first day of the retreat, an elderly Sister asked our group from Alameda, "How many of you young ladies would like to become Sisters? Please raise your hands."

Every girl except me raised a hand. I had no regrets. I felt more than a little rebellious and quite smug, thinking, "I will show those Sisters they cannot trick me."

Rebellion subsided, and my smugness melted as the second day progressed and I found myself having a serious conversation with my best friend, Jesus. I actually heard Him speaking to me, inviting me to come closer to Him, to walk in His ways in complete surrender. It came as an almost overpowering surprise, and I found myself wavering in Jesus' favor. He was getting through my veneer. The next day, I knew surrender was imminent. Many times during that day I heard myself saying, "Yes, Jesus, if You want me, I will serve."

The following months were not easy. I battled with myself, but could not come to a complete surrender. The latter part of my high school years found me a very confused teenager. There was scarcely any communication with my father—I seldom saw him more than once a month. My mother's advice to me during her life, and my obedience to my dad's admonition to attend Mass every Sunday were the things that kept me close to the Word of God, protecting me from temptation.

During my Alameda High School days, I continually prayed for my dad and regularly attended Missions and Novenas for his return to the Church. Once upon a time, he had been quite active in it, even serving as secretary for the Holy Name Society when he lived in New York. He was staying with a very devout Roman Catholic family and attending Mass with them, but he had not officially returned to the Church. There seemed to be a secret bitterness in him, a hurt he could not share. Aware of deep needs in his life, I always closed my letters to him with the words, "God bless you, and may you have the joy of everlasting life."

Meanwhile, my association with Lorraine Cardinet and her family developed into a close friendship. Mrs. Cardinet, although not a Catholic herself, constantly encouraged me to become a Sister. "You can at least give it a try," she would say. Four years later, she was baptized into the Roman Catholic Church, and two weeks after that she went to be with the Lord.

Almost constantly, I experienced an undeniable drawing to the religious life. I longed for a life of prayer, but any notion of becoming a Sister was still repugnant to me. Negative thoughts lodged in my mind, building resentment and hostility.

"You don't know anything about religion or Sisters," a little voice would whisper to me. "You have had no formal religious instruction. You wouldn't be happy in a convent. You're free. Stay that way."

That voice annoyed me until one day while I was in prayer, I heard

Jesus say, *I will lead you. I will teach you. Fear not.* Those words of assurance brought joy to my heart. No longer was there any indecision. I would enter a convent.

Right away, I went to visit my dad, to ask his blessing on my new life. Before I broke the news to him, we sat quietly, talking of other things, and I was emboldened to ask him about the burden he had on his heart.

"What's bothering you?" I asked.

During the long pause that followed, he had a faraway look, and I thought about what his life had been. Dad was not a tall man, but he had a wiry, athletic build. He was of German descent, with light blue eyes and a fair complexion that had presented quite a contrast to my Irish mother's black eyes and hair. I knew that he had always been a strong-willed person. When he was nineteen years old, my grandfather got a supervisory job for him with the Toledo, Ohio, Police

Department where grandfather was a detective. Dad stayed on the job only one day. He preferred learning a trade, he said.

He became a machinist, such a good one that he was never out of work, even during the depression years. After the sudden death of my brother from polio before my birth, dad was so broken up that he decided to leave New York City and relocate as far away as he could, as if moving could separate him from the sorrow in his heart. He and mother had moved to Alameda, California, with my two sisters. I was born later.

Dad had always been decisive. He made a decision and stayed with it. I wondered how he would react to mine.

When he finally began to talk, opening his heart to me for the first time in my life, he revealed his deep desire to have a son who would some-day become a priest in the Roman Catholic Church. His voice throbbed with emotion as he relived the birth of his son, believing that he would realize his greatest dream. But God had taken my brother home early. Then, when mother was carrying another child, dad was certain it would fulfill his dream. Instead, I had come along—

I knew dad loved me, but defeat was etched in every line of his face.

"Dad," I interrupted him, "dad, I'm going to become a Sister."

I watched as his jaw dropped and an expression that was almost a smile began to erase the sadness on his face.

"Well!" he said, brightening, squaring his shoulders. "Well! Maybe God is fulfilling my dream after all— almost— So you're going to be a Sister in a Catholic order!"

Dad's enthusiastic approval of my intentions cast from my mind all lingering doubts. But to make absolutely certain that Jesus was really choosing such a life for me, I put out a fleece.

"Dear Lord," I prayed, "if You really want me to become a Sister, then please keep me from becoming ill in any way during the six months of my postulant days."

It was a strange fleece, in a way, because I was so seldom sick. Was the Lord giving me a warning about what was to come? If so, it didn't enter my mind at the time, and I happily made my preparations to enter the convent.

Chapter 3
The Life of a Sister

I was not in the convent very long before I realized that Sisters were very ordinary people trying to attain a closer walk with God. I recalled what some of dad's friends had told me during one of my visits with him.

"Mary," one of them said, "you're going to be like a wild colt undergoing the restraint of reins for the first time." He laughed easily and then added, "I can just see you, a kid who has had so little discipline. You won't last long."

Another commented, "Rules and regulations will get you down, Mary. Three months is about all I give you. Then you'll be back here looking for a place to live and work."

They were partially right. There were times during those postulant days when I rebelled mightily. One day I was told that the novices were to present a skit. "This will not be a unified or teamwork effort," advised the Sister. "Each novice will give a small skit of her own."

I didn't want to put on a skit of my own. I didn't want to put on a skit with anyone else. I didn't want any part of a skit. I could feel rebellion building up inside. Seething with anger, I passed by a small concession display of donuts. For some reason, the display held my attention. I stood gazing at the donuts, and suddenly I had an idea.

"I'll do it. I will! I will!" I told myself, and burst into happy laughter. A Sister passing by paused, studied me momentarily, and then continued on her way, shaking her head.

The day for presenting the skits arrived. I watched the other novices make their presentations, wondering all the while if I dared to use the skit I had prepared. When my turn came, I hesitated a moment, and then my strong willpower asserted itself.

"I'm representing a salesman," I said. "I want you to think of me as a special type of salesman, selling a very special product—donuts." I paused, went through a few dramatic postures, accentuated by some steps from my childhood ballet dancing, and then continued.

"These donuts," I said, "are not the kind you eat. They are a special kind, what I call 'do nots.' We hear the phrase quite often here. 'Do not' do this and 'do not' do that. But always they're 'do nots.' "

Surprisingly, I was neither reprimanded nor questioned about my attitude. Perhaps the Sisters were well-acquainted with novices who did not adjust too quickly to rules and regulations after a rather free and spirited life.

There were other moments of rebellion, but as the postulant days progressed, and God honored my fleece by keeping me well, I determined to stick it out. In time, I developed a certain peace and satisfaction. I received many outward signs of blessings from God, such as the gift of tears and a deepening personal relationship with Jesus Christ. But once I received the white veil, at the completion of six months' postulancy there followed a struggle through a period of spiritual dryness which Saint John of the Cross has called "the dark night of the senses."

God seems to permit dryness and aridity in order to purify the soul. During these times, God tests the purity of one's intentions and sincerity of heart. Jesus tells us clearly,

"He cleanses and repeatedly prunes every branch that continues to bear fruit, to make it bear more and richer and more excellent fruit" (John 15: 2 TAB). In such days of spiritual trial, faith is increased, because one has to rely on and trust Jesus for every step.

When the training days and formal education required for Sisterhood were over, I was assigned to my first mission. With three other sisters, I was sent to a territory south of San Francisco. The diocese provided us with a convent, a small cottage, and a car. In addition, we were given ten dollars and one cooked meal as our initial sustenance. Beyond that, we were expected to beg for the upkeep and work of the mission.

We gave religious instructions to the young and the old. Our class-rooms were open areas in fields, under trees in an orchard, or space in a hall. We even held one class in an old, abandoned gasoline service station.

During those first months of teaching, I began to hear reports of Holy Rollers being jailed for disturbing the peace of their neighbors. I had no idea what Holy Rollers were. I did have a strange feeling that if they were worshiping the same Lord I worshiped, I didn't understand why they should be jailed. Although I prayed for them, I did so lightly. They weren't really a matter of deep concern to me—I had my own burdens as well as duties to perform.

Our convent was in a region of vegetable and fruit farms, and the farmers gave us all the produce we needed. One afternoon, we were given a considerable amount of fruit and vegetables and returned to our classes. Two days later, when one of the Sisters was driving the car, she asked, "What is that terribly unpleasant odor?"

Riding in the back seat, I looked all about me, but could find nothing. The next morning, as we were starting out for classes, the odor was almost unbearable. Trying again to find the source of it, I opened the trunk of the car, and received the full blast from a mass of beautiful but very odoriferous yellow mustard greens in full bloom. We had forgotten to take them out of the car the afternoon the farmer had given them to us. We never forgot mustard greens again.

Because we were at war with Japan, the Pacific coastal areas were required to be blacked out at night. One night we were awakened by the sound of tramping feet outside our little convent.

"Wonder what's up," I said.

"Guess there must be a party of some sort," a Sister replied. "It's of no concern to us, so let's go back to sleep."

We had not been sleeping too long when the telephone set up a terrible jangling that awakened us. "Who could be calling this time of night?" I asked.

"Probably some of those people we heard earlier," came the reply.

"Maybe they're inviting us to their party," I joked.

"Well, someone answer the phone," said another Sister.

I climbed out of bed, picked up the phone and said, "Sister Mary Bernard speaking."

"Are you Sisters still there at the convent?" came the surprised voice of our pastor.

"Why do you ask?"

"Haven't you heard? A Japanese submarine has been sighted off the coast. Everyone in the area has been evacuated to the hills. You are the only folks left in town."

I thanked the pastor, cradled the phone, and told the Sisters what our pastor had reported. An excited discussion followed over whether we should leave the convent or stay. We decided to remain and suffer whatever consequences might be in store for us. We did dress, however, then crawled back into bed and pulled the covers over us. The night was uneventful, and later we learned that the scare was caused by a false report of a submarine sighting in Monterey Bay.

Our little town soon became a collection of various communities of Sisters. We seemed to have led the way, establishing a beachhead for the others to follow. Six Sisters received permission from the Pope to come out of cloister and set up a new monastery in our town. One of my contacts with them was through acting as their chauffeur, driving them to Mass every morning for six months.

Our life was packed with action, but to show Jesus' love was always our first priority. I liked the way an anonymous poem expressed it:

Put ye on Christ—Be souls of
    prayer,
Build all on this—not here alone,
    or there,

But moving, whatsoever path be
    trod,
With heart and mind uplifted to
    your God.
Put ye on Christ our Lord the
    livelong day
In selfless labor, giving self away.
Choose not, reject not, but un-
    ruffled do
Whatever be your Father's will
    for you.
Put ye on Christ our Lord with
    souls at rest
Through all the toil because He is
    their Guest.
Let every thought and word and
    act increase
In all who touch you, gentleness
    and peace.
Put ye on Christ our Lord. The
    great lone Heart
That in the crowd of men dwelt
    still apart,
There is your strength, your
    prayer: Know ye 'tis good

To keep Christ's company in
   solitude.
Put ye on Jesus Christ. The friend
   so true
 Who says and does such tender
   things to you.
Glad in His love, scatter love
   abroad,
Because you are in love with
   Christ our Lord.

One day, about three years after I
became a Sister, I was saying the
Angelus, and repeated the last anti-
phon in the usual way: "Pray for us,
oh holy Mother of God, that we may
be made worthy of the promises of
God." As I heard myself say the
words, it suddenly dawned on me
that I did not know what the promises of God were. I opened the Bible
at once and began reading Saint
Matthew's Gospel, searching for His
promises. As I read, I was surprised
to find that there were so many
promises—more than I could keep up
with.

At about the same time, I came upon another anonymous poem which
was strangely meaningful to me:

Give me the faith that asks not
   "Why?"
I shall know God's plan by and by.
Give me the faith that looks at pain
And says, "Twill all be right again."
Give me the faith that clasps God's
   hand,
When things are hard to under-
   stand.
Give me the faith to bow my head,
Trustfully waiting to be led.
Give me the faith to face my life,
With all its pain and wrong and
   strife
And then with the day's setting sun,
I'll close my eyes when life is done.
My soul will go without a care,
Knowing that He is waiting there.

I couldn't have guessed how soon I
would need the faith that asks not
why, the faith that could bear unbearable pain, the faith to endure without
understanding.

All during the four years in my first mission, our little band of four Sisters were so busy teaching and helping others that it seemed there was no time for walking, not even to go to the post office to get our mail, much less to go for hikes around the country. Much as I loved to walk, it seemed the job of being chauffeur usually fell to me.

In January of 1944, I suffered a severe sore throat which developed into a flu-like condition. I was confined to bed, and on the second day, I was seized with a strange jerk-like feeling which seemed to center at the bottom of my spine. Suddenly my whole body stiffened and turned blue. A Sister came into the room and heard me crying out with pain, and I was rushed to the hospital.

After two weeks of hospitalization and various tests, the medical authorities concluded there was nothing wrong with me. However, my body did not agree. I felt quite certain that the sacrum, a triangularly shaped composite bone at the base of the spinal column, had been out of place but had shifted back to its normal position. My entire nervous system knew that there was something definitely wrong. Later, I learned that driving a car so much had caused my double-jointed anatomy to fall out of place.

In the meantime, my chauffeuring days were far from finished. A month after my hospitalization, I was transferred to San Diego to replace a Sister who had gone to be with the Lord. Upon my arrival, I met nine Sisters and an eccentric car which had been named Miss Lotta Rattles. She was a Ford, vintage 1929, and had been given to the Sisters fifteen years before my arrival. Miss Lotta never stopped going, not even when her parts were out of place.

Her main problem was a self-starter pedal which always stuck. Regardless of how we prayed, it refused to work. Eventually, I discovered from the Sisters that if we got out of the car and rocked her back and forth, the pedal would snap back into its proper place. Then we would jump into the car and take off, praying that it wouldn't stick again.

Miss Lotta Rattles loved attention, and she got it. No matter where we drove, people stopped and stared at us, often smiling at the antique we were using for our conveyance.

One day one of the Sisters and I went shopping not too far from our convent. When we had finished our chores, we returned to Miss Lotta Rattles for the drive home—but she refused to start. That afternoon, when the car wouldn't budge, I got out and began trying to rock it back and forth. But I wasn't strong enough to move it. A few people walked by, looked back, and were unable to control their laughter at seeing a Sister apparently trying to push an automobile all by herself. The scene was satisfactorily concluded when four young men from a nearby insurance office came out and applied their strong backs to the task. Miss Lotta Rattles could not resist such masculine strength, so Sister and I were soon on our way.

Nearly everyone in town wanted to buy Miss Lotta Rattles because, except for her one infirmity, she was in fairly good shape. Her motor and other parts were in acceptable operating condition. But structural parts do eventually wear out with age, and one day, Liz, as some affectionately called her, sprang several leaks in her roof. Liz was so indispensable to our operations that we had to postpone repairs until some future day when she would not be needed. In the meantime, on rainy days, the Sisters would hold umbrellas over themselves and over me as we drove about town, keeping relatively dry while the roof dripped like a sieve.

Each time before we took her out, even on short trips, we poured a gallon or so of water into Miss Lotta Rattles' radiator. Her gasoline gauge had worn out years before, so in addition to giving her a drink of water, we had to get out the little black book to see how many miles we had driven since we last filled the gas tank. We weren't allowed any mathematical inaccuracies or we would find ourselves drawing straws to decide which Sister would walk to the nearest gasoline station.

Eventually we got the self-starter, the top, the radiator, and the gas gauge repaired and decided it was time to send Miss Lotta Rattles off to a new home. A "For Sale" sign was attached to the inside of the back window. One day, when we were starting for town, several extra Sisters piled into the car, so Miss Lotta Rattles was quite crowded. When we reached our destination and the Sisters alighted, we all started walking down the street. Shrieks of laughter pealed from onlookers who saw one of the Sisters hustling along the sidewalk with the "For Sale" sign stuck to the back of her coat.

Miss Lotta Rattles' last journey was a memorable one. We had been visiting our absentee students when we came across a destitute family which needed immediate help. I reported the case to my Superior, and she immediately provided food, clothing, and other provisions, which we loaded in the back seat of the car. My Superior suggested I buy some fresh eggs in the country. On the way to the destitute family, I saw a sign advertising fresh eggs for sale and turned in the driveway. A young man appeared and asked how many dozen I wanted to buy. After the usual exchange of conversation, he peered into the back seat.

"What are you planning to do with all those things?" he asked.

I explained that we were taking them to a destitute family down the road.

"I know them," he said. "But they're not Catholic," he added, looking puzzled.

"I know that," I answered.

The young man was so overcome with our ecumenical disposition that he donated the eggs for the family from then on.

I learned later that the young man's father, Mr. Weber, had purchased a new truck and wanted it set apart and blessed. In thanksgiving for his goodness and generosity to the Sisters, we prayed, asking God's blessing and protection for the vehicle. The following week, Mr. Weber told me that he had been on his delivery route, and had stopped the truck to deliver some eggs to a customer. He thought that the front wheels were turned in the proper position so that if the brake gave way, the truck would merely roll to the side of the road and stop.

But when he returned from making his delivery, he saw his new truck loaded with eggs rolling down the hill toward a busy intersection. He stood in utter amazement as he watched the vehicle safely cross the intersection and ease to a stop against a curb in such a way that not a single egg was so much as cracked. Jesus had rewarded our prayers and Mr. Weber's faith and generosity with a miracle!

Similar wonderful and exciting incidents were frequently part of our everyday fare. But there was also a forewarning of more trouble for me. Pain had started in my lower spine, and it was increasing in intensity. Then, on the feast of Corpus Christi, I received a spiritual insight into my future years. While I was praying to Jesus, He seemed to convey to me these words: *I want you to suffer with Me.* I knew there were many kinds of suffering, and I could only wait upon the Lord for His revelation.

Chapter 4
An Endurance Test

Each year while I was in San Diego, the sacrum in my spine seemed to slip farther and farther out of place until at last it became impossible for me to walk normally. I was taken to doctors, and after being examined, would walk out in a worse condition than when I entered. Eventually, I was hospitalized again. All the doctors knew something was wrong, because I had no knee reflex, regardless of how hard they tried to get one. I had two weeks of hospitalization, and many x-rays were taken. Then, as before, I was dismissed with the words,

"We cannot find anything wrong with you." Nothing wrong with me! And yet I could hardly walk!

Preposterous, I thought. How could I go on? To whom could I turn? One week later found me still in a painful condition physically, and then another blow came—a letter informing me I was being transferred to another convent.

The trip to my new mission via the motherhouse in San Francisco was a rough one. We went by car, driving four hundred miles up the coast, leaving before dawn, and arriving after sundown. When we drove into the yard of the building where I was to wait to be taken to my new assignment, I thought my back would break in two, because I had been sitting so long. The pain was so intense that I went directly to the room assigned me. There, a two-day wait for Sisters to come for me from my new mission convent gave me time to think and to pray.

I reread the words from Hebrews 12:2-13 which I've always found so comforting. Those verses tell us to keep our eyes fixed on Jesus, the One who inspires and perfects our faith. He endured the cross, heedless of its shame, for the sake of the joy which lay before Him. We are reminded that if we respect our earthly fathers who correct us, we should submit all the more to our heavenly Father. God disciplines us for our true profit, that we may share His holiness. We are advised to strengthen our drooping hands and weak knees, to make straight the paths in which we walk so that our halting limbs may not be dislocated but healed. The words renewed my spirits—but not my body.

How much I wanted healing for my tired and aching body, but there was no healing. To make matters worse, my new Superior had not been told of my physical condition. She gave me one of the hardest teaching assignments in the Schools of Religion, the task of pioneering a new school located some sixty miles from our convent. In addition, I would be a companion to several other Sisters.

The task appeared almost insurmountable to me. I felt like an amateur mountain climber, looking at Mount Everest for the first time. However, I reasoned that "God makes all things work together for the good of those who have been called according to his decree" (Rom. 8:28), and there was no turning back. I plunged into my new work with all the energy I could muster, determined to learn how much more my spine could take. I had lost faith in doctors after my two futile hospitalizations.

The climax came on the day when my sacrum refused to take any more. It felt like a grater was being scraped up and down my spine, and the pain became so severe that tears rolled down my cheeks. There was still half a day to go before the end of the school day, so I began swallowing aspirin—two, then three, then two again, and then three. Finally, fourteen turned the trick. But there was no hiding my condition any longer. My Superior, realizing my condition, suggested I visit a chiropractor since I had no more confidence in medical doctors. I would willingly have seen a horse doctor if someone had suggested he could help me.

I was the chiropractor's first patient early the next morning. By this time, my spine had become so crooked that I had developed a considerable limp. The sacrum had been out of place since 1944, and this was 1953. In that nine-year period, the muscles and sacrum had become so accustomed to their altered position that when they were finally put into their proper place by the chiropractor, they screamed. So did I!

Despite the initial pain accompanying the adjustment, the day became a joyful one. I could actually walk normally once again. But the remedy was short-lived, because the muscles refused to hold the sacrum in its proper position. For three years, I visited the chiropractor's office almost daily. The words of Job came to mind so often: "Naked I came forth from my mother's womb, and naked shall I go back again. The Lord gave and the Lord has taken away; blessed be the name of the Lord" (Job1:21).

I found some others, however, who, in my eyes, were in worse condition than I, so I tried transferring sympathy for myself to them. One was Joe, the boy with muscular dystrophy. To know that he came to experience the loving grace of the Lord Jesus Christ and accept Him as his Savior was my Lord's assurance that my teaching in the School of Religion was His will for me. That assurance helped me to bear the excruciating pain which made me down a dozen aspirin daily.

The three years of constant manip-
ulating by the chiropractor kept me
walking, but often the sacrum would
be out of place for a considerable
time when it was impossible for me
to go in for treatment. I continued
living in the hope that eventually the
muscles would be strong enough to
hold the sacrum properly and secure-
ly; however, one day the chiropractor
told me there was nothing more he
could do.

Not satisfied with giving up, I turned to another chiropractor in San
Francisco.

"Your case is hopeless," he told
me. "I'm afraid your problem may be
a ruptured disc."

Back in my room at the convent, I
cried out, "Oh, Lord, what am I to
do? What is it You are trying to tell
me? You said You wanted me to suffer with You, but, dear God, to what
purpose?" My whole nervous system
was out of order, and I knew it.

I was aware that Jesus knew my suffering. He had suffered in so many ways for me. I drew encouragement and consolation from the Scripture in such passages as Romans 5:2-5:

Through him we have gained access by faith to the grace in which we now stand, and we boast of our hope for the glory of God. But not only that—we even boast of our afflictions! We know that affliction makes for endurance, and endurance for tested virtue, and tested virtue for hope. And this hope will not leave us disappointed, because the love of God has been poured out in our hearts through the Holy Spirit who has been given to us.

I also enjoyed a number of books about the saints—Saint John of the Cross, Saint Theresa of Avila, Saint Bernard, Saint Thomas of Kempis, Saint Catherine of Siena, and Saint Therese, the Little Flower. I felt I could identify with them in their sufferings, thinking I had really gone through the spiritual experience of the dark night of the soul. Ironically, God gives us this experience to produce humility within us, not pride. "Apart from me you can do nothing" (John 15:5).

In my own thinking, I had reached a peak of perfection, and it took the wisdom of my spiritual Mother to come to the rescue and save me from the pitfall of pride. For many months, when her Feast Day came on the religious calendar, I received a public humiliation of some sort. It happened so often that the words of Saint Bernard came to mind: "There is no humility without humiliations."

"Oh, God!" I exclaimed. "What kind of thoughts have I been having?" Not until after I realized my sin of pride and confessed it did the public humiliations stop. Blessed Mother had brought me back again to the feet of my Savior, Jesus, but still I was without hope of deliverance from my physical malady. One day between classes, my pain mounted, despite the aspirin medication. In tears, I limped from one class to another. A dear woman standing in the hallway saw me and wanted to know if I was in pain.

"Oh, I'm so sorry," I apologized. "I didn't see you. Please forgive me for succumbing to the pain in my spine and legs."

"You look just like my sister used to look, limping around, and in awful agony," the woman said. "She had gone to a chiropractor for three years. Eventually, the disc ruptured."

"What happened?" I asked, hoping her sister had received some remedy that might also be beneficial to me.

"She is better now—like a new woman."

"What happened? Who helped her?"

"She went to a wonderful nerve surgeon in Oakland who operated on her spine. Now she can bend and walk without pain. She feels twenty years younger."

A medical doctor who could help me! My heart leaped for joy. The woman gave me his name and address, and I could hardly wait until I reached the convent to inform my Superior. She was overjoyed with the good news and suggested I contact the doctor at once for an appointment.

After Doctor Lester Lawrence, a well-known neurosurgeon, examined me, he spoke with tenderness and sympathy. "You must have suffered a great deal, Sister." Corrective surgery was scheduled at once.

It was like a miracle! After the operation, I could bend and walk straight, with very little discomfort. I was living in a brand-new world! After twelve years of suffering, I finally had relief. My cup overflowed.

All went well until I tried to resume a full seven-day weekly schedule. After a few months of that, I broke completely. There was nothing wrong with my spine, but after so many years of suffering, my nervous system had gone awry.

I was transferred to the mother-house for a complete rest. It was winter, and the cold was damp and penetrating. Unaccustomed to doing nothing more than a few household duties, I wilted like a wallflower. The pain in my back increased, and my legs refused to support me. I clung to the walls as I walked. But in the midst of these physical adversities, Jesus had a spiritual feast awaiting me. It happened during a week I was left alone while the Sisters were attending a retreat in the convent.

At that time, a renewed interest in reading and studying the Scriptures was surging through the Catholic Church. I had just been given my first complete Bible, containing both the Old and New Testaments. With a week to myself, I began, for the first time in my life, to read the Bible from Genesis to Revelation. I can never thank Jesus enough for that rare treat in my life. I so felt the presence of the Holy Spirit on every page that I could be thankful for the disabilities that kept me from attending the retreat.

When the Sisters returned from the retreat, I was taken to a Catholic hospital where the house doctor examined me. He reported to my Superior that I had hypersensitive nerves, and suggested physical therapy at the hospital. After several months of this treatment, strength returned to my legs, and I felt normal again. Within two months, I was recommissioned to another convent south of San Francisco. It was a growing parish with an enrollment in the schools of close to one thousand students. As supervisor and coordinator in a new School of Religion,

It was my responsibility to keep things running smoothly and harmoniously among teachers and students.

One day, we learned that a blind man, believed to be molesting children near the schools, was sought by the police. Naturally, I was concerned, and that concern became a fearful nightmare when I discovered that a blind man had been engaged to teach in one of our schools. I obtained his name and address, and with a companion, I went to visit him. A friend of his greeted us at the door. "I'm sorry," he said. "The teacher is sick and is not having any visitors until he is feeling better."

I suffered for a week with the fear that the blind teacher was the man being sought by the police. Then the news media reported that the police had apprehended the child molester. A few days later, our blind teacher, having recovered from the flu, returned to his classes, and we became close friends. I learned that he had been a swimming instructor in a community near Los Angeles, and one day he had dived and hit his head on a concrete abutment, causing him to lose his eyesight.

While teaching ninth grade boys in one of our schools, he was attending Law School at Santa Clara University. He later finished law school, passed his bar examination, married, and joined the law department of a large firm near Santa Clara.

Another unusual person who came into my circle of acquaintances was Gladys West, who, after bearing three children, became the victim of polio. With a teacher companion, I went to visit her one day. A maid ushered us into the home. We were introduced to Mrs. West, a beautiful woman with lovely auburn hair, who was encased in an iron lung. She was lying on her back with a mirror above her head enabling her to carry on face-to-face conversations with people who came to see her.

She and her husband had been happily married for several years, but when polio struck, making her an invalid, he ran off to South America with another woman, taking the children with him. She asked the courts for custody of her children, won the case, and they were returned to her. Now the three teenagers were attending Catholic schools.

Mrs. West supervised the household, ordered the supplies for the family, directed the maid in her duties, and cared for, loved, and disciplined her children. Her parents assisted her financially, making possible the lovely home.

My association with the blind teacher and Mrs. West convinced me that my problems were merely small pebbles compared to theirs. My future was in the hands of Jesus, and I vowed to leave it there. But it is always much easier to make a vow than to keep one.

After six months on outdoor duty and three days a week in charge of sewing skirts and blouses for twenty-eight Sisters, I felt my legs begin to weaken again. Finally, they refused to support me, and I was taken to a doctor at another Catholic hospital. Again, with only a casual examination and no x-rays, the physical therapist informed my Superior that my problem stemmed from an emotional disturbance. My only comfort came from such Scripture passages as James 1:2-4, 12:

> My brothers, count it pure joy when you are involved in every sort of trial. Realize that when your faith is tested this makes for endurance. Let endurance come to its perfection so that you may be fully mature and lacking in nothing . . . Happy the man who holds out to the end through trial! Once he has been

proved, he will receive the crown of life the Lord has promised to those who love Him.

I knew I had entered an endurance test. No one seemed to believe I was in pain. I was actually told that I was suffering from neurosis. Relieved of my outdoor work, I was grateful to continue my sewing charge. At this point, the road was rough. Every day was a living nightmare of pain and misunderstanding. In essence, I was holding on to the knot of a swinging rope, just swinging back and forth in midair, not knowing what would happen next. Only the realization that Jesus loved me enabled me to cling to the rope, knowing that this mental, physical, and spiritual trial would not continue forever.

Who indeed can harm you if you are committed deeply to doing what is right? Even if you should have to suffer for justice' sake, happy you will be. "Fear not and do not stand in awe of what this people fears." Venerate the Lord, that is, Christ, in your hearts. Should anyone ask you the reason for this hope of yours, be ever ready to reply, but speak gently and respectfully. Keep your conscience clear, so that, whenever you are defamed, those who libel your way of life in Christ may be shamed. If it should be God's will that you suffer, it is better to do so for good deeds than for evil ones. (I Pet. 3:13-17)

I was assigned to the motherhouse again. It had been moved and now was situated in the country, nestled in the midst of a large estate that resembled a miniature Golden Gate Park.

I was not placed on duty fulltime, although occasionally I was sent back to my first mission as an emergency replacement for a Sister. Without so much pressure on my legs, they stopped paining, but each year I would have an acute attack of this mysterious ailment.

My new Superior suggested I return to Dr. Lester Lawrence in Oakland, the doctor who operated on my ruptured disc some five years before. He had some x-rays taken of my spine. A rather stoic man, he seldom revealed what was on his mind. But this day he pushed his stoicism aside.

"You have degenerative arthritis of the spine," he told me after studying the x-rays. "You will never be deformed, but this type of arthritis is most painful."

"Thank you for telling me, Doctor," was my only response. He didn't tell me that I would become bedridden, but he gave me medication to relieve the pain.

I had some active outdoor duty and enjoyed this time with the high school students. On Sundays, I conducted monthly Teenage Christian programs. There would be a Guitar Mass, a Christian speaker, and a social time afterward with live music. We heard about a popular Christian team at the University of Santa Clara, greatly liked by the teenagers, so we contacted and arranged a date for them in our program. I was told that the instigator and core of this Christian group was the president of the Santa Clara student body. What a joyful surprise when I met the young man. He was Greg West, the teenage son I had met previously when visiting the home of the mother in the iron lung. Her love, sacrifice, and fortitude in rearing her children had paid real dividends.

Thus life had meaningful compensations even though I was suffering physically. Whenever I had another attack of arthritis, the result was more medication and rest. Meanwhile, Dr. Lester Lawrence had died of a heart ailment, and I was referred to an arthritis specialist in a small town outside of San Jose. The attacks were coming more frequently, and I visited Dr. Siezbert hopeful that as a specialist he really could help me. He went over my past history, made a series of tests, and asked me to return to his office the following week.

That was one of the longest weeks of my life. I prayed almost continuously and fervently. The day arrived, and I walked into the doctor's office. His diagnosis was relayed to me in few words.

"There is no hope for your type of arthritis."

I rode home in tears.

Chapter 5
The Gentle Healing

Another summer, and with it came many eagerly awaited outdoor activities, including swimming in the pool which the Sisters enjoyed as often as their busy schedules would permit. As talk about swimming dominated almost every conversation, my thoughts turned to a Sister who many years ago had been completely paralyzed in an automobile accident. Her doctors said she would never walk again. However, continuous and persistent water therapy, although a slow process, returned her to normal health.

I decided that if such therapy helped that Sister, it might be useful in my battle against degenerative arthritis. For three months, I swam for forty minutes a day—two ten-minute intervals in the morning and two in the afternoon. Initially, I had to force myself into the cold water, but gradually I succeeded in extending the therapy periods, and after three months was so free from pain that I discontinued all medication. It was as if I had been transferred to an entirely new world. What a joy to find myself once again in a physical condition which afforded me the luxury of being of service to others.

Shortly after this newfound freedom from pain, I was sent as an emergency replacement to a mission convent in the little town of Camarillo, outside Los Angeles. Going south in winter is not always what people think. This particular winter was very severe. I joked with the Sisters, explaining that the cold would provide a good test for my arthritis. Surely if there was any arthritis left in my system, the sustained low temperatures would induce a relapse. I experienced some days when the cold Santa Anna winds seemed to blow right through me, cutting to the very bone marrow, but God was merciful. My back stayed all right. I returned to the mother-house without any ill effects.

A few months later—on Good Friday—the dread ailment attacked again, nearly doubling me over with pain. It became necessary for me to resume medication just to be able to walk. I said, "Oh, Lord, how can I complain? It's Good Friday." My thoughts went back to our Lord's severe struggle in the Garden of Gethsemane and His suffering for me. I didn't complain. I tolerated my condition and offered my services again for the missions. The Mother General gave me a choice of three convents. I selected one in the country, where I had previously lived. I knew it had a heated swimming pool for use during the winter. That convent also afforded me the pleasure of renewing old acquaintances among students and teachers. Life became a pattern of teaching, extra rest, and swimming. During Mass one Sunday, I saw Patty, a former pupil whom I had not expected to see again.

She was eleven years old and playing on the street when I had first met her.

"Why aren't you in school?" I had asked.

"They don't want me," was her honest reply.

"Where do you live?"

"Just down the street."

"Is your mother at home?"

The question seemed to upset her. Her little face took on a fearful expression, and she ran home. From townspeople, I had learned where she lived. After class that day, I visited her home to learn if I might be of any assistance. Patty was a retarded child who lived with her grandparents. They invited me into their scantily furnished apartment, and unfolded the story of Patty and her small brother whose mother had been convicted of cruelty to them. Court records revealed she had beaten the children many times, and the court had awarded the custody of the children to the grandparents.

"Wouldn't you like to have Patty attend our school?" I asked.

"Do you think she could learn?" the grandmother asked. "You know, the public school refused to accept her."

"I think Patty could attend our first-grade classes. At least we can give it a try." The grandparents' faces showed their appreciation and joy over the prospect of Patty attending school.

We had a picture book of Gospel stories for the little ones in the school, so I informed my Sister companion of Patty's circumstances and advised her about special treatment for her in class. By showering her with love and kindness, we would likely see improvement of her little mind and heart. Patty had responded beautifully, memorizing little prayers, and finally realizing that someone truly loved her exactly as she was. Every Sunday at the Children's Mass, she sat next to the Sister who taught her, drinking in everything she heard.

Encouraged by Patty's progress, one day I asked her a few questions about Jesus and herself. Her little face beamed with love for her Savior. Satisfied with her answers to my questions, and with her attitude, I decided the child should not be denied receiving Jesus in Holy Communion. I told the priest I thought Patty was ready to take Holy Communion. He gave no def'nite reply, so taking silence as consent, I told Patty's grandfather that she would be included in the First Communion Class and would be questioned by the priest very soon. He bought Patty a new white outfit for her important day.

On the day of the test, the priest told me that Patty was not to receive Jesus. He had never worked with retarded children, and was afraid she would do something wrong, not intentionally, but just from not knowing what she was doing. My heart sank. I didn't know how I would break the news to grandpa but finally sent him a note explaining the circumstances. The next day, the priest came to me with the startling news that he had changed his mind about Patty. "She can go through with the First Communion Class," he said.

Patty looked like a little angel as she received Holy Communion. A few days later, I learned from her grandmother why the priest had changed his mind so quickly. When grandpa had received my note, he had gone directly to the rectory where he had confronted the priest and warned him, "Father, if Patty no receive Jesus in Holy Communion, I burn down your house. I do not change my mind. You give me the answer *now!*"

Patty not only had the joy of Jesus' acceptance of her, but when the next term started, the school received her as a pupil in the third grade. She advanced in her studies and was able to take care of her grandfather after her grandmother passed away. This was the same Patty, now grown to womanhood, attending Mass that Sunday morning so many years later. We had a good visit.

"I'm still thanking Jesus for accepting me as I was," she told me as we parted.

There were other parishes where, though I was not a resident, I taught elementary and junior high school classes. In one sixth grade class, I had assigned the students to visit a Jewish synagogue and a Protestant church. Each student was to report on his visit, and a class discussion would follow. Only three of the students carried out their assignments, so I postponed it to a later date. That evening, as I was thinking about the failure of the class to follow my instructions, a gentle voice within me asked, *Did you go to a Protestant service?* I immediately went to the telephone and contacted two Protestant friends. The following Sunday, they drove me to their church. As we were going into the two-story structure, I noticed the sign outside: "Shiloh Temple." It sounded Jewish to me, but I asked no questions. Once inside, I noticed everyone with open Bibles. On one wall of the church, in large letters, I read, "That we all may be one." Reading that took my breath away, because in my prayers for many years I had been asking Jesus to make us all one.

The congregation stood and sang a hymn, singing from their hearts, and I thought how hard it is for our Catholic parishioners to open their mouths during Mass. Then they started to clap their hands as they sang, and they looked so joyful. We were free to clap in class or at a Guitar Mass, but not otherwise. Then, suddenly, the congregation began to worship God in a manner I had never heard before. There were voices speaking strange languages I could not recognize. Amidst the many voices, I felt the presence of the Holy Spirit. As a young Sister, I had a special devotion on the indwelling of the Blessed Trinity, and I could sense the same Divine Presence now that I had felt then. I was familiar with the ministering of the Holy Spirit, and I knew that He was present.

When the service ended, I realized I had heard nothing contrary to Catholic doctrine. Everything taught at the service was straight from the Scripture, just like our little catechisms. And everyone was so friendly. They called each other brother and sister. I was introduced to some

Catholics who were present, so I did not feel out of place.

Some time later, it dawned on me that this must have been a Pentecostal service. In no way did I connect this group with the Holy Rollers that I heard about many years before. My friends gave me some books to read, including *They Speak with Other Tongues*, by John Sherrill. I had read the epistles of Saint Paul many times and recalled that he considered "tongues" the least of the gifts of the Holy Spirit, so I tucked the book away in a box in my room.

The message on the banner in Shiloh Temple, "That we all may be one," remained in my mind, reminding me of a Scripture in Ephesians:

> This means that you are strangers and aliens no longer. No, you are fellow citizens of the saints and members of the household of God. You form a building which rises on the foundation of the apostles and prophets, with

Christ Jesus himself as the capstone. Through him the whole structure is fitted together and takes shape as a holy temple in the Lord; in him you are being built into this temple, to become a dwelling place for God in the Spirit. (Eph. 2:19-22)

I really believed that all Christians one day would exemplify a spiritual oneness in the Body of Christ. I longed for this day and kept the plea constantly in my prayers.

Meanwhile, another school year was nearing an end when another acute attack of arthritis struck my spine and hospitalized me. Sisters nearly always have the luxury of private hospital rooms, but I felt this was not practicing holy poverty, so I asked to be placed in a four-bed ward. The second day of my hospitalization, I was put in traction, and the doctor gave me a shot to kill the pain. My body immediately rejected the medication, and I began to vomit continuously, until I was so dehydrated that I had to be fed intravenously for a week.

In the midst of my distress, the doctor stormed into the ward and shouted at me, "Why didn't you tell me?"

"Tell you what, doctor?" I asked, mystified.

But there was no explanation from him. Curious, I watched other patients as they returned from surgery, expecting them to go through the same ordeal I had suffered, but they didn't. After I left the hospital, I learned that my body had passed the toleration point for some medications. If I continued taking them, I would again go through the same reaction I had experienced in the hospital.

After a week in traction, I was able to walk again. But in my heart, I knew this was the last time I would be working in convent missions. In May, 1968, I was transferred back to

the motherhouse to face the unknown future with a crippling disease. Once again, I turned my attention to others and began calling on
patients in rest homes.

There were so many who needed
help. One man of Mexican descent
was admitted during one of my visits,
but I did not see him again for several
weeks because he was kept in his
bed with the curtains drawn about
him, closing out all visitors. One day
I accidentally bumped into his bed
and heard an agonizing groan. I
peeped through the curtain and looked upon a little man curled up in bed.
I pushed the curtain aside, went to
his bedside, clasped his hand, brushed his hair and brow, and waited.
Finally he looked up, saw that I was
a Sister, and his face, which had been
so forlorn, burst into a radiant smile.
I asked him if he spoke English and
he shook his head no. I continued to
speak in English, combined with
some crude Spanish that I thought

no one could understand; however, he nodded at the right times. The nurse found me holding his hand and said irritably, "That man can't understand you."

"Why that's strange," I replied. "We've been conversing for fifteen minutes."

It was wonderful to see his reaction to a little thoughtfulness and kindness. His health improved, and soon he was wheeling himself around in a wheelchair. When he expressed a desire to receive Jesus in Holy Communion, I told the Father, and after that, the man received Holy Communion every month.

When the Billy Graham film, *For Pete's Sake*, came to the San Francisco Bay area theaters, I volunteered to serve on a committee to sell tickets. I considered it one way to demonstrate my Christian ecumenical spirit, and I was surprised to encounter opposition. Calling on a Christian drug-abuse center, I asked, "Would you like to have some of the boys see the Billy Graham movie, *For Pete's Sake*? It's truly a worthwhile movie."

"We don't need that sort of thing around here," replied a priest, acting as spokesman for the group. All Sisters and priests do not react as he did, however; I saw quite a few of them at the showing I attended.

When Billy Graham himself came to the Oakland Coliseum, I attended two meetings. One night, after the meeting, I failed to find the family who brought me, but fortunately met friends who offered to drive me to the motherhouse. On the way, they stopped at a restaurant for a snack. I knew this would make my arrival at the motherhouse late. Ordinarily I would have worried, but I didn't because a voice said to me, *Don't be concerned. Everything will be all right.*

It was 12:45 when we arrived at the motherhouse, and I knew the door was locked. I prayed the dogs would not bark and awaken everyone. I didn't want to ring the doorbell and wake all the Sisters either. Again that gentle voice spoke. *Knock on the door.*

"That's nonsense," I told myself. "No one will hear me." But I did knock, and almost immediately, I heard footsteps, and the little chain on the door began moving.

"Who is it?" a voice inside asked quietly.

"It's Sister Mary Bernard."

The door opened, and there stood my Superior. I nearly toppled over with surprise. She closed the door. "I woke up just as you knocked on the door. I didn't know you were out."

I had told another Sister to tell the Superior, but she evidently forgot all about it. "I went to hear Billy Graham," I explained.

The Superior smiled knowingly. My late arrival was all right, just as God had assured me it would be.

A few months after starting my rest home apostolate, I had another severe attack of spinal arthritis. Sister Superior thought it best that I return to the hospital for another bout in traction. After I was wheeled into the hospital, the thought occurred to me that perhaps I could rent a home traction outfit and undergo the treatments without hospitalization. I asked the doctor, and he not only consented but directed Sister Superior and me to a store where such rentals were available. I could not walk from the car into the store, but a clerk came out with crutches, and I received my first instructions on how to walk with them right there on the sidewalk. Instructions were also given me on how to attach the traction unit to a bed.

The doctor said that I should be in traction every morning and afternoon at different times. Crutches provided my only means of mobility. But I couldn't reconcile myself to just lying in bed between meals and swimming therapy and otherwise doing nothing. I phoned the head supervisor of the amputee ward of the Naval Oaknoll Hospital in Oakland, explained my circumstances, and asked if I might write to some of the boys who never had visitors or could not visit their homes. The supervisor came to the motherhouse and gave me the names of some of the boys to whom I might write.

My new venture developed into a delightful exchange of letters with these boys, and I was grateful for this new apostolate which made the hours speed by. Meanwhile, I visited an orthopedic doctor in a nearby town. After examining me and all my x-rays, he said, "You are not to sit down anymore."

"But, doctor, how am I to eat? Off a mantelpiece?"

"You are not to sit down, not even when you go to the bathroom." He was serious.

That was a new one. I had experienced unusual conditions in the past, but I never thought it would come to bathroom gymnastics. I had to smile, despite the seriousness of the situation.

"I suggest you purchase a bar stool and sit on the very edge. In doing this, there will be no pressure on your spine," he explained.

I had slept on boards, on the floor at times when the pain was most severe, but now I was to sit—or not-sit—perched on the edge of a bar stool!

There were many hours during the next few weeks when the pain was almost unbearable. If it hadn't been for Donald, a retarded boy who painted very well and visited the motherhouse, I could not have endured the mental and physical agony. I asked Donald to paint a picture for me of Jesus with His crown of thorns. Don-

ald had experienced mental suffering, since many people had rejected
him in various ways, and his own
sufferings were actually pictured in
Jesus' face. My own union with Jesus'
sufferings grew during this period.
I learned the literal truth that it is
only in dying to self that we come to
know the whole Jesus:

> I solemnly assure you, unless the
> grain of wheat falls to the earth
> and dies, it remains just a grain
> of wheat. But if it dies, it pro-
> duces much fruit. . . . If anyone
> would serve me, let him follow
> me; where I am, there will my
> servant be. (John 12:24,26)

Despite my condition, there were
times when I was able to hobble
around on crutches. I also had visitors. One Sunday, a lady I had met
at the rest home called on me with a
friend from Australia. After the usual
amenities, they began asking me
about my arthritis. I replied jokingly,

"Oh, that's my ticket to heaven. I have to have something to get in with."

The lady from Australia replied, "You know, Sister, I would not be here today unless I had received a miracle for my own back trouble."

I brushed aside her words with, "Oh, but this is God's will for me."

"Who told you that? Who said it was God's will?"

The question stunned me, because we Catholics never think of it in any other way. Was not this the cross that Jesus told us to take up and carry?

The lady asked, "Did you ever read in the Gospels where Jesus ever made anyone sick. No! He said, 'I am come that they might have life, and that they might have it more abundantly' " (John 10:10 KJV). Next, she quoted from Isaiah 53:5:

> But he was pierced for our offenses, crushed for our sins. Upon him was the chastisement

that makes us whole, by his
stripes we were healed."

"Why don't you ask Jesus for a
cure?" the woman asked me.

"Oh, I could never do that," I replied. "In the first place, I'm not de-
serving of it."

She smiled. "Neither was I. You
see, Jesus is very merciful. He knows
our worthlessness, but He loves us
anyway."

Then both women got to their feet,
and my friend from the rest home
said, "We have a little prayer group
in our church on Tuesday mornings.
We will include you in our prayers
this coming Tuesday."

"Thank you very much," I said.
"I just can't ask God for a miracle.
But you can pray."

They smiled and left. I quickly
went upstairs to my bed, more than
exhausted from standing on crutches
during the visit. But they had given
me much to think about. I wondered
why Catholics didn't ever think about

what these visitors had told me. I could never get up enough courage to ask for a healing miracle. Was our traditional mentality and Catholic teaching keeping me from something that Jesus had promised? Did He really want me to be bedridden for the rest of my life?

One thing I did know. I was not to be enclosed within four walls. It was not that *I* minded it, but such confinement would make it difficult for me to communicate Jesus' love to others. I knew that love as a child. And when I was a teenager, Jesus had invited me to a closer walk with Him. Then, during my years as a young Sister, it became total surrender to Him. Later, He spoke those prophetic words to me in San Diego: *I want you to suffer with Me.* By now, I had been through many years of physical and mental suffering and spiritual agony. Nevertheless, the words of Jesus always confronted me—those words in

John 6:67: "Will ye also go away?" (KJV). I knew I could never go away from Jesus. I wanted to go all the way with Him.

I would answer Jesus as Peter did: "Lord to whom shall we go? You have the words of eternal life" (John 6:68). I would not falter in my love for Him, but if I were closely confined, I would miss spreading His Word to others.

The following morning, I had another conversation with Jesus. "Dear Lord," I said. "I know that You can heal me. I have no doubts about that. But is it Your will?"

I asked for an outward sign as I had in the beginning of my religious life. Since I had recently started writing letters to amputees among our war veterans, I asked the Lord to make His will known to me in the presence of one of those letters. I let the entire matter rest there, knowing the Lord would honor my request.

The next day was Tuesday, and I went about my activities as planned, completely forgetting that my visitors, who had been so certain of Jesus' will to heal me, would be praying for my healing. After my swimming therapy in the late afternoon, I lay face down and began writing to an amputee. I finished the letter, placed it in an envelope, and sealed it. Then, still holding the letter in my hand, I grabbed my crutches, pulled myself up, and started to walk. Then it happened! The crutches suddenly began to burden me. I let them drop to the ground. I tested one step. Then another! And another! I could walk! Glory be to God! In my hand I was holding the outward sign—a letter to an amputee. I recalled, too, my friends who had said they would be praying for me.

"Oh, dear God, I did not even ask You for a healing. You, in Your mercy, knew my need."

I will never forget the date and hour—September 23, 1969, at 5:15 in the afternoon. The strength had returned to my legs. Unconsciously I bent down, trying to see what had happened to the muscles in my right leg—they had been bulging almost through the skin. The bulges had disappeared completely! Then I realized I was bending over. "Oh, God," I exclaimed, "I'm bending!" It had been months since I had been able to bend at the waist.

I stood perfectly still, gazing heavenward, bathed in God's divine presence. It was not the first time I had felt the Lord so near me. As a young Sister at the motherhouse, I had seen a light that looked something like a tongue of fire behind me, and I had distinctly felt the Lord's presence. Then had come the encounter—the indwelling of the Blessed Trinity—when His presence had permeated my whole being in a glorious shaft of light.

Reflecting now on these beautiful experiences, I understood why in my younger days Jesus afforded me such an intimate relationship with Him. He knew the intense sufferings I would endure in His divine plan of purifying and refining the metal of His spouse's love.

I recalled the words of Judith in the Apocrypha:

> Besides all this, we should be grateful to the Lord our God, for putting us to the test, as he did our forefathers. Recall how he dealt with Abraham, and how he tried Isaac, and all that happened to Jacob in Syrian Mesopotamia while he was tending the flocks of Laban, his mother's brother. Not for vengeance did the Lord put them in the crucible to try their hearts, nor has he done so with us. It is by way of admonition that he chastises those who are close to him. (Judith 8:25-27)

I had been healed through the divine power of the Great Physician, my Lord. Prayers had been said for me the very morning of the day of my healing. What wonders prayers have wrought!

In my ecstasy, I gave no thought as to *why* the Lord had healed me, but in the days ahead I would learn He had very definite work for me to do, feeding His flock in distant pastures.

Chapter 6
A Higher Spiritual Plane

Providentially, perhaps, my next appointment with Dr. Ruth was scheduled for the day following my miraculous healing. I walked into his office, and he immediately noticed I was without crutches. "Why, Sister," he remarked, "you're quite agile this morning."

"Oh, yes," I replied. "However, before you examine me, I would like to ask you one question. Do you mind if I give all the credit and glory to God?"

He smiled without taking his gaze from me. "You know, Sister, as well

as I, that He is the Divine Physician.
I only prescribe. He does the healing.
'Give thanks to the Lord, for he is
good, for his mercy endures forever'"
(Ps. 118:1).

How wonderful it was to drive the
car again and to walk without crutches. As I drove to the motherhouse, I
thought of my father. It had been so
long since I had seen him. I received
permission from the Mother General
to use the car for a full day, so I called
dad and asked him if he would like
to attend a musical on Sunday at
Sigmund Stearn's Grove in San Francisco. He would. When we arrived at
the grove, there was not a parking
place to be found. However, I was not
to be defeated so easily, and decided
the driveway to the city reservoir
would provide ample space. I knew
parking was prohibited there on
weekdays, but since it was Sunday,
the reservoir road would not be used.

"Just in case I should get a ticket,

dad, you pay the fine," I teased. He agreed, and we hastened to the musical. The performance was delightful, and when it was over, I led the way to where I had parked the car, but it was not there. At first, dad thought I was teasing him, but then my consternation registered with him. He suggested we telephone the police and report the car stolen.

We tried several houses before we found anyone at home. A very kind gentleman made the call for us, because my teeth were chattering so from fright that I couldn't talk. The police wanted to know the license number, make, style, and year of the car. After a few minutes checking, the officer said the car had not been stolen but had been towed away from the reservoir driveway because it was illegally parked. The man who had made the call for me considerately drove us to the police station, ten blocks away, to make arrangements for repossessing the car.

After signing the necessary papers at police headquarters, dad and I took a bus across town to the garage where the car had been towed. I presented to the attendant the papers the police officer had given me. After dad paid a $13.50 tow charge, the attendant returned the papers, saying, "You'll need these, Sister." I tucked them in my purse and drove to dad's favorite Chinese restaurant, where we enjoyed a delicious dinner.

Once back in the motherhouse, I was happy to be in my own room. It had been a delightful day, inconveniences and all. As I went through my purse tossing out inconsequential things, I was about to discard the papers from the police department, but decided, instead, to keep them as souvenirs. They remained on my desk for about a week, when, once again, I concluded they were of no value and started to toss them out — but a little voice within prompted me to read them. One of the papers was a receipt for $13.50. The other was a parking ticket calling for a $15.00 fine! I took it as a warning not to disregard public laws in the future.

Shortly after this escapade, I began attending a Scripture course at one of the nearby parishes. It wasn't long before I realized that the people present did not appreciate the priest's theological explanations. They wanted the Word of God made more relevant to their everyday lives. It was the old story of the priest talking over the heads of the parishioners. The fault rests primarily with the seminaries which saturate the seminarians with theological statements and expressions that lay people don't understand. Jesus gave the apostles and disciples explicit directions: "Teach them to carry out everything I have commanded you" (Matt. 28: 20). I can't find anywhere in Scripture where Jesus said, "Teach the theological and philosophical aspects of My Word."

I became newly convinced that *practical* teaching was needed, and soon after, the Lord led me through a telephone call to teach the Word of God to a group of adults. A lady at the rest home phoned one day and asked if I could explain a passage of Scripture to a friend. I agreed to help. She and her friend became the nucleus of my first Bible class. Meanwhile, I started attending a prayer group at a Catholic church and learned that many of those present knew nothing about Scripture. For members of this group, I started a second Bible study class, with permission from my Superior.

I was happy to instruct Catholics who had been long deprived of the beauty and knowledge found in the Word of God—deprived because an erroneous idea had developed through the years that we must have a theologian explain the Bible to us before we can open the Book. One Sunday, a Catholic couple visited me, and I told them I was giving Scripture lessons to adults. The husband exclaimed, "Oh, but we can't just read the Bible for ourselves. We can't understand it."

"I'm sure," I replied, "that you would never want to place yourself in this category." I opened the Bible to II Peter 3 and read verses 15 and 16 aloud:

> Consider that our Lord's patience is directed toward salvation. Paul, our beloved brother, wrote you this in the spirit of wisdom that is his, dealing with these matters as he does in all his letters. There are certain passages in them hard to understand. The *ignorant and the unstable* distort them (just as they do the rest of the Scripture) to their own ruin [italics mine].

I went on to assure the couple that
they could trust God to keep them
from misinterpreting what they read.
Jesus made that clear when He said:

> If you live according to my teach-
> ing, you are truly my disciples;
> then you will know the truth, and
> the truth will set you free. . . . Not
> by bread alone is man to live, but
> on every utterance that comes
> from the mouth of God. (John 8:
> 31-32; Matt. 4:4)

"Clearly then," I said, "we are to
read the Scriptures, all of them, and
to live by their truths as God reveals
them to us."

What a joy were those months of
teaching! At intervals, I managed to
attend Shiloh Temple to fellowship
with the congregation there. My two
Pentecostal friends called on me occasionally, and we would always
discuss Jesus and His Word.

Meanwhile, the year was speeding
by. Holy Week arrived, and the moth-

erhouse scheduled a retreat led by a Benedictine priest. It was impossible for me to attend the retreat because of other duties, but the following Monday, in passing the Community Room, I saw a notice on the table. It read:

Suggested reading material for
Sisters who made the retreat—
The Cross and the Switchblade
  by David Wilkerson
Catholic Pentecostals
  by Kevin and Dorothy Ranaghan
They Speak with Other Tongues
  by John Sherrill
Face Up with a Miracle
  by Don Basham

How interesting, I thought. I already had *The Cross and the Switchblade* and *They Speak with Other Tongues*. I had tucked them away in a box long ago. Within a few days, two sets of all four books were placed on the table for anyone to read. Curiosity and a deep desire to learn more about the Pentecostal movement spurred me to read all four books.

It was a few days before Pentecost, and I was nearing the end of the final book—*Face Up with a Miracle.* I almost envied Don Basham as I read of his experience with the power of the Holy Spirit. Why couldn't I receive as he did? I read on, and he suggested you and I could receive on our own.

"Oh, no, Sister Mary! You couldn't do that! You're not worthy." I stopped short. Why should I tell myself such things? I called one of my Pentecostal friends of the Shiloh Temple congregation.

"Sheila," I said, "I have just finished reading some wonderful books. Could you come over this Sunday, Pentecost, and pray for me? I want the Baptism with the Holy Spirit like the Apostles, the Blessed Mother, and the disciples had."

"How delightful," she said, and stopped short. Then, in a disappointed voice, she explained, "I'm so sorry, but I have to be at church this Sunday. Would next Thursday be all right?" I tried hard not to sound dejected as I agreed to the following Thursday for her visit. It would still be the octave of Pentecost.

I had only a few pages left to read in Basham's book. I finished it Pentecost eve. As I read those final pages, a deep surge of longing and love entered into my heart, and I found my pillow wet with tears. Jesus' love had welled up within my breast to overflowing. My heart yearned so much for Jesus to baptize me that I decided, unworthy or not, I would do as Don Basham suggested. I would get out of the boat like Peter did and walk in faith on the waters toward Jesus. With that in mind, I fell asleep.

For years, the Feast of Pentecost had been my favorite feast day. In the Catholic liturgy, it is not an historical day like Christmas or Easter, but a day of the living Presence of the Holy

Spirit in the Church, signifying the mystical Body of Christ—all Christians united under one Lord. As I always held a deep devotion for the Holy Spirit, as a Sister, Pentecost was a day of deep significance for me.

After an inspiring Mass in honor of the Holy Spirit, we finished our prayers, and then the whole Community gathered in the dining room for a special sumptuous breakfast. But my mind and heart were not on the food. I managed to keep up a good conversation with the Sisters, all the while hoping breakfast would end more quickly than usual.

Finally, breakfast over and the dishes out of the way, I dashed upstairs to my room, closed the door, and locked it. I did not want any unexpected visitors, because I was ready to get out of the boat and walk on the water in faith.

The bar stool I had used during my spinal troubles sat in front of my

desk, facing the window. I hopped up on it. The first requisite, I recalled, was to praise the Lord. How I loved it when the whole congregation at Shiloh Temple raised their hands in worship and praise to the Lord. They were not bashful or reticent to give honor, glory, and praise to the Almighty God. Neither should I be, and so I began to voice my inner thoughts of love and thanksgiving in audible English. Soon, I ran out of thoughts of my own, and opened my Bible to Psalm 103, giving praise to Divine Goodness, and Psalm 104, giving praise to God the Creator. In faith, I was walking on the water. Finishing my song of praise, I stopped. "Lord where do I go from here?" I asked. I began flipping the pages of my Bible, not knowing where I would stop to read. The pages fell open to the *Song of Songs.*

I had read them before, but now when I came upon the words "sister" and "bride," a strange, warm feeling came over me. I continued to read, and my heart became so immersed in God's love that the tears began to flow. I completed all eight chapters and then burst forth into a language I had never heard before. I continued to praise in this beautiful, strange tongue for some twenty minutes. I grasped the significance of the gift of tongues that Pentecost morning in my own room — *the upper room*.

I recalled the words of Isaiah:

> I rejoice heartily in the LORD, in my God is the joy of my soul; For he has clothed me with a robe of salvation, and wrapped me in a mantle of justice, like a bride-groom adorned with a diadem, like a bride bedecked with her jewels. (Isa. 61:10)

From that day on, I entered into a new dimension of God's power and love. During my religious life, I had been known as a person of joy and laughter, but now everything was enhanced with my new experience in the Holy Spirit.

I opened a letter that Father Wilfrid had sent me just a month before. Many thoughts had crossed my mind concerning the Holy Spirit being present at Shiloh Temple in Oakland. How could the Holy Spirit be present in these different churches and in our Catholic church too, especially when we taught a few basic doctrines that were different? In fact, it puzzled me so much that I had written Father Wilfrid about it, and this was his response:

Benedictine Monks
St. Pius X Monastery
Pevely, Missouri

April 21, 1970
Dear Sister Mary Bernard:
Thank you kindly for your letter. Praise the Lord over the fruitfulness He has wrought during the Holy Week Retreat.
There is no denial of the differences of doctrine between the

various Christian churches. But this does not keep the Holy Spirit from working within those churches, and showering their adherents with the outpouring of His many gifts.

Vatican II says that the Holy Spirit works in the heart of any good man of good will, even though he may claim to be an atheist—attaching him in some mysterious way to the Body of Christ.

If the Spirit does this, what is there to prevent Him from working within the lives of all those who believe in the Lord Jesus, even though, owing to historical circumstances, they are divided on some points of doctrine?

And must we Catholics also not admit that we too have not been wholly faithful to the full truth of the Gospel? And yet we believe that the Holy Spirit is at work in our Catholic tradition.

Is not the Spirit teaching us that before there can be unity of doctrine there has to be a greater unity of faith in Jesus and a unity in a life of prayer, under the Word of God, and under the direction of the Spirit?

What we need most of all is the power of the Spirit. You say you now long for the baptism of the Spirit. Then accept Jesus as Savior and Lord of your life, pray to Him for the outpouring of His Spirit, keep on hungering for the Spirit. Jesus will lead you to a fulfillment of your prayer— through your prayer, and most probably through the prayer of other Spirit-filled Christians. Do keep me in your prayers, as I will you, for all your present intentions. Ever in the Spirit of Jesus,
Father Wilfrid

Father Wilfrid did not realize that I had known Jesus personally ever since my First Communion days. How thrilled he would be to know Jesus had baptized me in my own room on Pentecost Sunday. It wasn't long before I wrote him, relating the good news and how it happened.

The Scripture courses I was teaching became a spiritual springboard for me. I rejoiced verbally by expounding on how wonderful Jesus is in His great love for all mankind. Word of my enthusiasm in my deeper spiritual life spread among my Sisters, and soon they were saying I had become a fanatic. The Superior one day, in all seriousness, cautioned me, "Sister, you must watch yourself."

"Why?" I asked. "What have I done wrong?"

"Oh," she replied, "you're talking entirely too much about Jesus. You know, you really sound like a fanatic. The other Sisters are talking. You cannot and will not be allowed to attend any more prayer groups as you have done in the past." She stopped abruptly and turned away from me.

I was shocked. I rushed to my room, where again I felt the Lord's divine presence. It was as though His arms were around me, and He was saying, *Don't cry, child. I will give you all the fellowship you need in the future.* That was just like Jesus. I calmed myself and thought how beautiful and personal is His concern for us, even to knowing our need for fellowship.

Knowing that my Sisters and Superior were not aware of Who I had received, or what a spiritual experience had been mine on Pentecost, I managed to control myself in their presence. If they didn't like to hear about Jesus outside of their religious instruction classes, surely they would not appreciate the beautiful experience I had on Pentecost Sunday.

I had been told not to attend any prayer groups, so I obeyed the order.

But Jesus provided something far more beneficial. Every month, I attended an all-day session of the Inter-Church Renewal in Oakland, where the Holy Spirit was in full power. The sessions not only provided fellowship and instruction, but enlarged my acquaintance with people of various denominations. One of these acquaintances was Rudy Moreno, a former drug pusher, heroin addict, and prison frequenter. He was a changed man when I met him.

Rudy had heard about Teen Challenge in San Francisco from a former drug addict. "Maybe this is a way out of hell for me," he said, and tried Teen Challenge. There he learned of the tremendous love, mercy, and power of Jesus Christ, and he became a new creature. However, his beautiful wife, a nominal Catholic, was not experiencing this wonderful life in Jesus. Rudy brought her to see me one day, and we talked about the

Scriptures. Later, she joined my Bible class. After several lessons, she confessed to me that she had suffered terribly from migraine headaches ever since she was a teenager. Knowing the power of Jesus, I suggested we pray together for her physical and spiritual healing. We did, and her faith began to grow. Within a few weeks, she met Jesus in His Word and found a very personal relationship with Him, becoming a new woman spiritually and physically. Her migraine headaches disappeared, and her love for Jesus equaled her husband's love for Him. They read the Scriptures together at home, united in mind, heart, and spirit.

One evening, a bewildered and perplexed mother rang the doorbell of the motherhouse. She had come to see me about a family problem. Actually, she had several problems. Among her six children, one twelve-year-old boy had made a number of attempts at suicide, and two sons in their early teens were involved in shoplifting, drugs, and alcohol. This was supposedly a good Catholic family. They attended Mass and Holy Communion every week.

I invited the distraught mother to come to my Scripture classes, and suggested she bring her husband. After a month of personal instructions and follow-up, they joined a prayer group, as well. The prayer groups had been praying for the boys ever since the mother first contacted me.

We believed Tony's behavior was possibly caused by demon oppression. Ever since he was a child of three, he had been given to violent tantrums at home. Later, he exhibited the same behavior in school. The mother admitted that her own temper had very little calming effect on the son. During our sessions, it was also revealed that Tony experienced a dreadful emotional setback during his third year when he saw another three-year-old boy so severely burned that he died.

Eventually, the parents and all six children were attending the Inter-Church Renewal meetings. Here, each member of the family came to know and accept Jesus Christ as Lord and Savior, knitting them closer together as a family group. Then they began seeking the Baptism in the Holy Spirit, and each received the Baptism either at the Inter-Church Renewal or in their home. Suicide, drugs, alcohol, and shoplifting were things of the past—gone forever.

My various activities left me little time for leisure, but I managed to keep in touch with dad, and I received permission to attend his ninetieth birthday party. Ever since his full return to the Church one year on the Feast of the Holy Family, we had grown increasingly close.

Knowing dad's fondness for candy, I stopped at a wholesale candy distributor to buy his favorite sweets. There I met a woman who was helping her husband in the candy business. Her hands trembled as she waited on me.

"Is there something wrong?" I asked her.

Her eyes filled with tears as she told me that her oldest boy was in prison on a drug-pushing charge. We were alone in the store, and I suggested we pray for God to lessen her burden. We held hands as I entreated God to remove all stain from this woman's life through the Blood of Jesus Christ who gave His life for our sins.

At the finish of my prayer, the woman seemed greatly relieved and asked me to continue to pray—for her and for her son, too. I promised, and said I would visit her again. I visited her many times, and after her son was released from prison, I had the privilege of leading him to Jesus Christ. How many blessings we receive in our day-by-day lives when we are alert to others' needs and minister Jesus to them.

At dad's party, I sat next to a man with his leg in a cast and a drink in his hand. He had been run down by a motorist. By the time he was on his fifth cocktail, he had become very talkative. Dressed in my black habit, I represented to him "the established Church," and soon I became the target of all his religious gripes. Because he was not defaming any specific person with his hidden hatred, I listened to his tirade. I, too, had met Catholics—laity, Sisters, priests, monsignori, and bishops—who were not setting good examples for others.

"I agree with you," I said, in all honesty.

He was so surprised that all he could say was, "You do?"

"Yes," I answered. "I know human nature very well. You see Jesus Christ is head of the Church, and if we don't attach ourselves to Him, we are worthless. Jesus gives us the true picture in John 15:5: 'I am the vine, you are the branches. He who lives in me and I in him, will produce abundantly, for apart from me you can do nothing.' "

Before the evening was over, the man confessed that he had lived a very sordid existence for years and wanted to return to the Church. I leaped for joy inside and quickly told him I knew a good priest who could help him. A week later, the priest joyfully told me that the man had contacted him, made a cursillo, and with his wife, accepted Jesus into his life in a very personal relationship.

A few weeks later, friends from Shiloh Temple, a Dominican Sister, and I went to the Temple's summer camp, known as "Springs of Living Water." It was the old "Richardson Springs" of years ago. The services were spiritually uplifting, and what a contrast my Dominican Sister and I provided—two Catholic Sisters among four hundred Pentecostals. This would not have been possible a few years ago. But the prayer of Jesus is coming true: "That all may be one" (John 17:21).

During one worship service, the Reverend Costa Deir read a passage from Saint Paul's letter to the Corinthians (I Cor. 11:17-32) concerning our dispositions before receiving the Body and Blood of Jesus. He spoke to the congregation of the necessity of being in harmony with one another. If anyone had any grievance or bitterness against anyone else present and was not willing to forgive, he or she should depart. Several did so.

The minister exhorted the rest to express their reconciliation to their brethren who might be in need of it. A pregnant woman in a row ahead of me knelt in front of another woman. Some were shaking hands, and others were embracing each other. I began to choke up inside, and tears moistened my cheeks. What an impact it made on me—so many forgiving one another before the Commu-

nion service. How many Catholics I
know brag about going to Mass and
Holy Communion every day but have
not talked to their neighbors for
months, sometimes for years. Gossip
and lies are their usual conversation
over their backyard fences.

> Forgive us the wrong we have
> done as we forgive those who
> wrong us. . . . If you do not for-
> give others, neither will your
> Father forgive you. (Matt. 6:12,
> 15)

The time at "Springs of Living Water" was memorable, filled with His
love and joy, and fellowship with
those we loved. He was preparing me
for the opening of new avenues for
feeding His sheep.

Chapter 7
Encounter with Demons

One day I opened my Bible and read, "I was ill and in prison and you did not come to comfort me" (Matt. 25:43).

For years I had considered this verse in the Bible to have spiritual application. I had taught others how to love Jesus, but according to this verse, did I actually know what He wanted me to do, especially about the people in prison?

"Lord," I said, in all humility, "if I can be led, please let me do something about the people behind prison walls."

The next day I met a Catholic chaplain from Soledad Prison who said Mass for us occasionally. I told him of my desire to write to prisoners. He said he would see what he could do. Two weeks later, I received a long letter from one of the Soledad inmates. He had written the letter to the chaplain, who had forwarded it to me. After leading a life of degradation, sin, and misery, the poor man wanted to find some way out of his humiliating situation. He asked the priest if he could find a mature, churchgoing woman, a handicapped person, and a young child to whom he could write. It might take some time to find three persons meeting his exact specifications, so I teasingly replied to his letter, asking if I would do until he found the others.

He responded immediately, stating I would fit all three categories. I knew he needed a steadfast friend, so I introduced him to the Word of God, where he could find a personal friend in Jesus. In time, I found a family interested in writing to this prisoner. The mother of the family was a churchgoing woman. She had a retarded son and a teenage daughter.

One day, the mother telephoned me. She wanted me to go with her to visit her daughter, Rose, in a hospital in Stanford. We drove to San Jose to have lunch with her daughter-in-law whom she wanted me to meet also. After lunch, I asked the woman if we were going to the hospital to see Rose.

"No," she replied, "Rose is having brain tests today. We can't see her."

I learned that Rose had been a somewhat strange child, whose behavior puzzled the family. She was unusually gifted in music and especially drawn to those in need. When she reached high school age, she began to suffer from dizzy spells and epileptic seizures. Her friends in the Catholic school she attended suspected that she was on drugs. The girl had made several suicide attempts and was presently hospitalized for psychiatric treatment.

"You know, Sister," the mother finally tearfully confessed, "about two years ago, Anton Lavey, director of a satanic house in San Francisco, was on a television program. Rose saw it, and she started writing to him because she was a Christian and thought she could convert him."

"She has been corresponding with him ever since?"

"Yes."

"I know what is wrong with your daughter. I've heard of these cases before."

The mother was startled at my blunt statement, but would not consent to my visiting Rose. We drove home in silence, but a few days later I telephoned the hospital and contacted Rose. She said she would not mind if I came to see her. I invited a lady whom I had met in the Scripture course to go with me. She also knew the girl. I told the mother of our plans, and she asked to accompany us.

While we were talking with Rose, her mother excused herself and went to talk with a nurse, I presume, about her daughter's condition. I seized the opportunity to ask Rose the all-important question: "Have you ever written to Anton Lavey?"

She readily admitted corresponding with him, explaining that he had sent her his black blessing. "Ever since then," she said, "I have been physically ill, and the doctors cannot find out what is wrong with me."

Rose's mother returned then, and I questioned her no further. I knew enough. We were crossing the Bay Bridge on the way home and the mother confessed that at times she had felt like jumping off it.

There was no doubt in my mind that Rose was suffering from demon possession. The demon had to be exorcised. I telephoned several Catholic priests, but all made excuses. Why were they afraid? Did they not know the power of Jesus? As a teacher of religion, I taught students that with the power of the cross, holy water, and the name of Jesus, one could drive the devil away. Suddenly, I remembered a Pentecostal minister and his wife who had exorcised a demon from an acquaintance of mine, and she had been greatly relieved. I contacted the pastor, and he agreed to see Rose. Two weeks after the pastor and his wife performed the exorcism, the girl was released from the hospital and returned to her home.

A few weeks later, I had a strong premonition that something had happened to Rose. A check with her mother confirmed my suspicions—she had slipped back into demon possession. I called the minister who had cast out the demon, and he advised me to seek the aid of a Spirit-filled priest in San Jose. He was out-of-town, so I called another Spirit-filled minister, and he asked me to bring Rose over to his house immediately.

The meeting was a face-to-face encounter with demonic powers. The minister, who was experienced in such ministry, listened as I tried to help Rose by explaining what she had told me in the hospital. To my surprise, she contradicted everything I said and called me a liar. Realizing we had reached an impasse, the minister sent the daughter and her mother from the room.

"Sister, this is a case of repossession," he explained. "She does not want to be delivered this time, whereas before, when you saw her at the hospital, she did. There is nothing we can do until she is willing to be helped."

The case seemed hopeless, but I determined to wait upon the Lord, knowing that in His own good time, He would bring to pass that which He desired.

In the meantime, strange things had begun to happen to me. After my Baptism in the Holy Spirit, I was told to practice my gift of tongues, to use it often. Each day while taking a swim in the pool, I would pray in tongues. No one could hear me except Jesus. It was wonderful, but after a while, doubts began to assail me. Was this for real? The more I prayed in tongues, the stronger became the assailing doubts.

One night shortly after midnight, I awoke from a sound sleep to discover I was not alone in my room. I sensed an evil spirit. Surprised and startled, I forgot my formal Catholic teachings: the sign of the cross, holy water, and the name of Jesus. I did, however, remember my gift of tongues.

A visiting Sister was sleeping in the next room, and only thin walls separated us. I did not want to awaken her, so I put the sheet over my head and whispered in tongues. Suddenly, without warning, I lowered my sheet, sat up in bed, and bellowed out two sentences in tongues. I recognized the name of Jesus as one of the words. Then, reminded of the power in the name of Jesus, I said, "In the name of Jesus, I command you, evil spirit, to leave this room."

I fell asleep immediately. The next morning, I thought possibly I had been dreaming, but when I met the visiting Sister, the expression on her face told me my experience had been no dream. I never again doubted that my gift of tongues was authentic. Since that night, I have not been a-fraid of any demonic attacks, because I know the power that will drive them away.

Not many days afterward, there was a surprise return of my old spinal problem. I sank to the floor, helpless, and finally raised myself to my feet by clinging to a chair. I managed to get over to the wall and found I could walk by holding on to the railing. That night in bed, I started to read

Prison to Praise, by Merlin Carothers (Logos). As I read, it dawned on me that God had healed me in a wonderful way. Would He now strike me down in pain? No, that would be a contradiction. The thought came crystal clear. This was not from God. I had been tricked by the devil. Satan got his walking papers then and there. The next morning, I jumped out of bed a new and well woman in Jesus. Alleluia! Praise His Holy Name!

My dentist had his office around the corner from the convent. When I went to him for my next dental checkup, I spoke briefly to his dental assistant. She told me she had just moved in next door, and asked if her five-year-old son might come to the convent grounds to see the beautiful flowers and lovely statues. I assured her he would be welcome anytime.

Shortly afterward, she and her son visited me, and I gave them a special tour of the grounds. When our conversation turned to her family, she told me that she had twins, a teenage girl and boy, who had been hearing strange noises in their bedrooms. Their beds actually shook at times, and they felt they were being watched.

"Do you think it could be an evil spirit?" she asked.

I was quite certain an evil spirit was involved, and she wanted to know what could be done. I made arrangements to call at the home that evening. In the meantime, I called a Spirit-filled Christian friend who was experienced in casting out demons and evil spirits. He gave me detailed instructions as to how to proceed with the exorcism. While considering the situation, I remembered something about a woman who had lived in the house for many years. Her son was driving home one night under the influence of alcohol. He had hit a telephone pole at the side of the driveway of the home and was killed.

That evening, while talking to the twins, I decided they were well-balanced children, not given to being easily frightened or to wild imaginings. They agreed with me that an evil spirit lurked in their bedrooms. I had fasted during the day and prayed, and I had brought a Bible and a bottle of holy water with me.

"You know, dear friends," I said, "only Jesus Christ can drive away evil spirits. Each of you must accept Jesus as your Lord and Savior and live according to His commandments if you hope to be free from visitations by evil spirits."

They assured me that they had already accepted Jesus. I then explained to them that as we visited the various rooms, they would hear me speak in something that sounded like a foreign language or unknown tongue. "It's a gift from Jesus, and very powerful in expelling evil spirits," I said. "However," I added, "I will also speak in English. You join me, repeating the English words after I say them."

I opened the Bible to Ephesians 4:26-27 and explained that first of all, they must forgive everyone who had offended them if they wanted Jesus to cast out evil spirits:

> If you are angry, let it be without sin. The sun must not go down on your wrath; do not give the devil a chance to work on you.

Together we read Ephesians 6:10-17 which tells us to draw our strength from the Lord, and to put on the armor of God so that we may be able to stand firm against the tactics of the devil. Paul explains that our battle is not against human forces, but against the principalities and powers, the rulers of this world of darkness, the evil spirits in regions above.

Then we read from I Peter 5:7-9:

Cast all your cares on him because he cares for you. Stay sober and alert. Your opponent the devil is prowling like a roaring lion looking for someone to devour. Resist him, solid in your faith, realizing that the brotherhood of believers is undergoing the same sufferings throughout the world.

After the Scripture readings, we visited every room, closet, hallway, and stairway in the house. As we entered an area, I spoke in tongues, sprinkled holy water about, made the sign of the cross, and said in English, with the family joining me, "In the name of Jesus Christ, I command all evil spirits to depart from this room, never to enter again."

At the close of the exorcism, all felt peace in their hearts. The mother had told me that the former owner of the house visited them each week, but always remained in the yard. In parting, I warned them not to allow her to come in the house, because she might bring evil spirits with her. A week later I called the mother. She said that no member of the family had heard or sensed any evil spirit activity since the exorcism.

My thoughts went back to the repossessed Rose who had become so depressed and uncontrollable that she had been placed in a mental hospital. I thought about her house, wondering if evil spirits might be present there. I telephoned Rose's mother and told her what I had encountered in the house near the convent, explaining how Jesus had driven the evil spirits out. The mother invited me to perform the same exorcism in her home. Going there immediately, I found Rose's room in a chaotic mess, with clothing and other things strewn wildly about. Rose's mother said that no matter how often she set things right, something somehow disarranged them again.

I understood why when she started unfolding a story she had never told any other person. When she and her family first moved into the house, prior to Rose's birth, they learned that murder weapons had been buried in the backyard. After the discovery, the mother harbored uneasy feelings about the house. I knew then why Rose did not have a chance for complete recovery when she returned to her room from the hospital. Evil spirits lurked there, waiting to repossess her. Jesus says in Luke 11:24-26:

> When an unclean spirit has gone out of a man, it wanders through arid wastes searching for a resting-place; failing to find one, it says, "I will go back to where I came from." It then returns, to find the house swept and tidied. Next it goes out and returns with seven other spirits far worse than itself, who enter in and dwell there. The result is that the last

state of the man is worse than the first.

After the demons were exorcised from Rose's house, and she herself was delivered again, she became a normal, happy teenager.

A woman attending one of my Scripture classes told me that she was having trouble in her home. She did not know the source of the problem, but I noticed that she often spoke about a very holy sister who visited her frequently.

"I would like for you to meet my sister," she said. "She is very beautiful. And I would like for you to meet my teenage son, too. I just cannot do anything with him. I feel there may be an evil spirit within him or in my home."

The day I visited her home, her son had gone to visit his grandfather, but her sister was there, occupied with some chore which kept her from knowing that I had come to rid the house of any evil spirits. However, I found none within the house, to the great relief of the mother. But in talking with the sister later and in seeing her illegitimate baby, I sensed that she was not of God. Her attitude, moral values, and conversation about her life proved the validity of what Jesus had said: "By their fruits you shall know them." As I talked with the woman later, she became convinced that the problems with her husband and teenage son stemmed from the presence of her so-called holy sister. The devil was using her to cause dissension, friction, and interference in her own marriage and family life. When the "holy" sister was not allowed in the house again, the woman's problems dissolved, and harmonious family living replaced the strife.

While vacationing for a week with friends in San Jose, I met a mother who asked if she could bring her eighteen-month-old son to see me. She was near a nervous breakdown, her marriage rocky, and she believed the youngster to be the cause of the problems. I agreed to see what I could do, if anything, and the mother brought the little fellow to see me. He looked for all the world like a cherubim, with curly brown locks and beautiful features.

"He has never been able to sit normally in a high chair. He has to be tied in," the mother told me. "He behaves like an animal."

I stood behind the child and said, "Lord, You brought me another case. You are the One who can do what is needed." Placing my hands upon the child's upper arms, I called upon Jesus to rebuke and cast out the evil spirit. The little fellow kicked, hollered, and screamed.

"Oh, Lord," I said, "teach me what to do, since You have given me this child." Then, remembering my gift of tongues, and leaving my hands on the boy's arms, I spoke in tongues for a few moments. At that point, I received an inspiration to repeatedly rebuke the devil in Jesus' name until the child went limp. After about five rebukings, the little fellow relaxed. That night, for the first time in his life, he sat on his mother's lap as she ate her dessert.

When I told the mother about exorcising the evil spirits from two homes, she asked that I come to her home to determine if such spirits existed there. Her Catholic husband rebelled against the idea of a Sister doing such a thing. He said that was something for a priest only. But he was considering blessing the house, and I assured him that one does not bless people or houses until they are free from evil. He consented.

Inquiring about former occupants, I was told that a drug pusher and his wife who had been convicted of crimes and imprisoned were the previous occupants of the home. Their child, who had slept in the same room as this eighteen-monther, had been too unruly and self-willed to discipline. Finding evil spirits in abundance in the crib room, I followed the same procedure of Bible reading, prayer, and devil-rebuking as I had used in the other houses. There were no more problems caused by evil spirits in that home.

The tactics of the devil, whatever form they take, are always destructive. We should instruct, enlighten, and even admonish, as Saint Paul points out in his letters. But we have no right to condemn persons. Jesus says:

> If you want to avoid judgment, stop passing judgment. Your verdict on others will be the verdict passed on you. (Mat. 7:1-2)

Chapter 8
Little Miracles

God was performing miracles, using me as an instrument through which the power of His Son Jesus Christ was manifested. I had no power to work these miracles, and I knew it. I wanted everyone to know and understand that. It was only by the power of Jesus Christ, sent through the Holy Spirit, that the sick were healed, marital problems solved, and demons exorcised. And I myself received additional healings.

One day I was trying to thread a needle. I was wearing my glasses, but my eyes failed to focus, and I couldn't see the eye of the needle. I thought I would have to see about getting stronger lenses. Then came an afterthought. "Did not Jesus heal me? Couldn't He heal all of me?" I knew He could.

"Dear Jesus," I said. "You healed my spine. I now implore You to heal my eyes. Thank You, Jesus. Alleluia! Praise You, Jesus, praise You." With those words, I *claimed* my healing and took off my glasses.

At first, I could not read a word when I looked into the Bible or my Breviary. But eventually, God restored to me a normal reading and sewing vision. I am still reading and sewing without glasses. Periodically, since childhood, I had been bothered with granulated eyelids. Shortly after discarding my glasses, I was affected by the return of that affliction. Again, I looked to Jesus with a prayer for complete healing.

"No more boric acid washing for my eyelids," I pleaded, and Jesus heard me. My Jesus is used to working miracles for His children. What He can do for me, I know He will do for others, because I have watched His healing power at work.

The parents of six children can testify to what Jesus did in healing their family. One Sunday, I noticed that one of the boys was wearing a patch over one eye. I asked what was wrong, and the mother explained that he had a bad eye, and the doctor was treating it by keeping him from using the eye.

"Don't you believe that Jesus can give your son new sight?" I asked.

She said she did and then added, "But, Sister, it had never occurred to me to pray about it."

The boy joined us in prayer, and afterward, his faith was so great that he ripped the bandages from his eye and exclaimed, "It's all right. Now I can see." He ran off to play.

After prayer, a young daughter began to experience the healing of a skin disease, the mother praised God for relief from an asthmatic condition, and the father ceased to suffer from the effects of hay fever. The healings were not immediate in every case, but they were real. The mother also began praying for children in her neighborhood. Two teenagers were healed of hay fever and allergies. A boy became a new person in Jesus, overcame emotional problems, and began sharing His love with others.

In each healing I have witnessed, faith has been an important factor. When faith is weak, I have seen healing falter. I was on a picnic one Sunday with friends when we happened upon a young girl who was spastic. She was walking across a rustic footbridge with the aid of French crutches. When I saw that she was having difficulty in keeping her balance, I rushed forward to help her. Recognizing my denomination by my religious habit, she struck up a conversation which resulted in her spending the remainder of the day with my friends and me. Her parents were picnicking in another part of the park. The little girl wanted to keep in touch, so I gave her my phone number.

A few weeks later, she came to visit me with a friend of hers who had great faith. The friend and I prayed for the girl, and she began taking steps about the room without her crutches. We were emboldened to take the youngster out into the garden where, holding my hand, she walked around the grounds without her crutches.

"This is the first time in my life that I ever walked alone," she exclaimed.

When it was time for her to leave, we walked to her friend's car. "I will get your crutches if you promise me not to use them anymore," I told her.

She bowed her head and replied, "Oh, Sister, I could not live without them."

I knew the girl who walked in the garden without crutches would not walk again without them—unless she built her faith in Jesus Christ as the Divine Healer. My thoughts returned to my own healings, gradual but lasting, and I exclaimed as the car drove away, "Thank You, Jesus. Thank You for everything."

One afternoon, a student in one of my adult Scripture classes invited me to fly with her to Los Angeles to attend a Kathryn Kuhlman service.

The morning of our flight, I noticed a woman with braces on her legs and a withered hand walking about in the air terminal. She was with a group going to Miss Kuhlman's services. I learned she had been to the services three times.

"Did you want a healing?" I asked.

"Yes, Sister. The first time I was there they told me to take off my braces, but I didn't want to."

"Why not?"

"I guess I didn't think I could be healed."

Again I praised the Lord for the faith He had given me for my healing and for the healing of others.

That afternoon, I sat at the Shrine Auditorium in Los Angeles with nine thousand people of all denominations and backgrounds. The service began with a two-hundred-voice choir singing beautiful and inspiring hymns. Then Dino, a talented pianist, and Jimmy McDonald, an excellent tenor, helped to lift our hearts and minds to God. When Miss Kuhlman walked on the stage, the very presence of God filled the auditorium. First, she asked those who were deaf to come up on the stage. Then she called for all those with back trouble.

"That doesn't mean me," I told myself. "I was cured a year and a half ago."

But Miss Kuhlman repeated, "I want all those who have ever had spine or back trouble to come up on the stage."

I knew then that it did mean me. I felt embarrassed and tried to convince myself not to go, because there was nothing wrong with me. But it seemed His gentle voice was saying, *Go up! Go up on the stage.*

I went.

What a thrill it was to be a part of this spiritual renewal in the Holy Spirit! But I felt nothing, no physical sensations of any kind.

That night, for the first time in many years, I awakened to find myself lying on my back without any pain. Another healing! Previously, I had not been able to lie comfortably on my back or to kneel for an extended period. Today, I delight in lying on my back, enjoying the wonderful realization of feeling no pain whatsoever.

A few weeks later, I learned I was to be transferred to the mission where I had spent my early novitiate. Before the transfer, however, I spent a beautiful day with the family who had experienced so many miraculous healings. Driving through the redwoods, we stopped at an Assembly of God church where we were warmly greeted. We gave our testimonies of God's wonderful goodness to us. Afterward, we remained to visit with members of the congregation, which included a number of Catholics.

I could say with the Psalmist:

> I will give thanks to the LORD with all my heart in the company and assembly of the just. Great are the works of the LORD, exquisite in all their delights. Majesty and glory are his work, and his justice endures forever. He has won renown for his won-

drous deeds; gracious and merciful is the LORD. (Ps. 111:1-4)

Two days after the picnic, my Mother General called me into her office and informed me that it was not the Community's practice to speak in other churches. I immediately suspected that one of the Catholics at the Assembly of God church had reported to the Mother General my participation in the service. I admitted that I gave my testimony for the honor and glory of God. Then I asked, "But, Mother, do we not say the Morning Offering every morning and try to live according to it?"

"Yes," she answered, gazing quizzically at me.

"And doesn't it mention that we pray for the intentions of the Sacred Heart (Jesus) for the salvation of souls, reparation of sin, and the unity of Christians?"

"Yes," came the answer again.

"Then if I pray for something,

Mother, what is wrong with trying to put it into practice?" She had no answer for that question, so I continued, "This is an opportunity for me to explain to you what I told the Assembly of God congregation. All this wonderful new spiritual experience came to me through Catholic circles. It was an assignment in our own Catholic Religion Books that told us to attend a Protestant service, which I did. It was then that I first became acquainted with the Pentecostal experience. The next incident, Mother, was when you invited a Spirit-filled priest to come to the convent and hold a retreat. Through his suggested reading of certain books, I encountered in my own room on Pentecost Sunday morning the fullness of Christian living. Now I am thanking God every day for it."

I stopped talking, because I could sense my Mother General's whole attitude had changed. She understood.

Quickly then, I asked her for permission to visit the same church the following Sunday to hear a Catholic priest speaking there.

"It would be all right with me, Sister Mary," she replied, "but I think it would be too soon, especially since our priest was so disturbed by your actions last week."

I thanked her and left, praising God for giving me the opportunity to witness to my own Community of Sisters who considered me rather eccentric in loving Jesus.

Within a week, I had received an invitation to speak to a group of high school students who had been studying the religions of the world and were currently studying Catholicism. I found that the teaching they had received on the Catholic faith was erroneous and biased.

"We all must remember that Jesus is the head of the Church," I told the students. I explained that if we take our eyes off of Him and His Word, many human discrepancies creep in. Catholics understand that the Pope acts as a visible head of the Catholic Church, just as other denominations have their visible heads. All heads of all denominations are human, and the Catholic Church is no exception.

I told them that just as Paul tried to teach the men of his day in his letter to the Corinthians, God shows us His way today through His Word. But all do not follow, because some teachers misconstrue the Word. Jesus tried to make it so lucid, so simple, that even a child could understand. His closing remarks in the Sermon on the Mount point to the need to obey His Word:

> So every one who hears these words of Mine and acts upon them—obeying them—will be like a sensible (prudent, practical, wise) man who built his house upon the rock; And the rain fell and the floods came, and the winds blew and beat against that

house, but it did not fall, because it had been founded on the rock. And every one who hears these words of Mine and does not do them will be like a stupid (foolish) man who built his house upon the sand; And the rain fell, and the floods came, and the winds blew and beat against that house, and it fell; and great and complete was the fall of it. (Matt. 7:24-27 TAB)

Addressing the high school students constituted my last actual witnessing for my Lord while at the motherhouse. I moved to a convent with some regrets—leaving old friends always brings some sorrow—but soon I was involved in a number of activities at the new home. I took the place of another Sister who had been visiting rest homes, and the Mother General gave me permission to conduct Scripture courses.

What better place to find prospects

for my courses than at a charismatic prayer group? I called a Catholic mother I had met several months before at an Assembly of God prayer group. She directed me to a prayer group in an adjoining parish, and it wasn't long before I began attending their meetings. There were Catholics there who were desirous of knowing more about the Scriptures, and soon I had a full schedule of Bible courses underway.

One day I spoke to a priest who, I thought, had received the Baptism in the Holy Spirit. I expected to have spiritual fellowship with him. When I told him about my miraculous healing and the Pentecostal experiences Jesus had so graciously given me, he looked at me in awe and said, "Oh, how I would love to be baptized in the Holy Spirit."

"You mean that you haven't had the Pentecostal experience?" I asked, surprised.

"No. Will you pray for me, Sister?"

We bowed our heads for a moment as I praised Jesus. Then I prayed for him. After the prayer, he admitted that the Holy Spirit would be a great help to him in preparing the sermons he was to deliver at a retreat. During that evening, I prayed again for the priest, wondering why he had not already received the Baptism. He seemed so eager for it— A few evenings later, I learned why. The priest taught seminarians, and to help them to receive good grades, he had taught them how to hypnotize themselves!

We cannot depend on magical arts and then expect the power of the Holy Spirit to help us. These are in opposition to each other. If we want Jesus' help, we must rely on Him and trust Him exclusively.

The Old Testament emphasizes that all practices connected with idolatry in any form are an abomination in the eyes of God. Saint Luke points out in the Acts of the Apostles:

Many who had become believers came forward and openly confessed their former practices. A number who had been dealing in magic even collected their books and burned them in public. When the value of these was assessed, it came to fifty thousand silver pieces. Thus did the word of the Lord continue to spread with influence and power. (Acts 19:18-20)

Saint Paul expressed his thoughts on the subject when he told the Hebrews:

Take care, my brothers, lest any of you have an evil and unfaithful spirit and fall from the living God. Encourage one another daily while it is still "today" so that no one grows hardened by the deceit of sin. We have become partners of Christ if only we maintain to the end that confidence with which we began.

When Scripture says, "Today, if you shall hear his voice, harden not your hearts as at the revolt," who were those that revolted when they heard that voice? (Heb. 3:12-16)

One day a Catholic mother offered to drive me home from a Scripture class. During the drive, I asked her if she had heard of the Pentecostal experience. She said she hadn't, and when I proceeded to explain it to her, suggesting she would find accounts of the experience in the Acts of the Apostles, Saint Paul's letters, and the words of Jesus in John's Gospel, she replied that it sounded interesting, but she had little time for reading. A few days later, she asked for my birth date.

"Oh, my birthday is past," I jokingly replied.

"But I'm serious," she said. "I really would like to know."

"Don't tell me you're in the astrology business," I teased.

"Very much so," she answered. "I make charts for people."

"I'm sorry," I said, "but I don't believe in horoscopes. It's a form of idolatry. I trust God for my future, not his creatures."

The woman was too deeply involved in astrology to break away, but before she started work on an astrology chart, she lit candles and said the rosary for protection. I am certain there was little protection for her from our Blessed Savior, because He told us to rely and trust in Him. In Acts 7:42-43, we read:

> But God turned away from them and abandoned them to the worship of the galaxies in the heavens. So we find it written in the Book of the Prophets: "Did you bring me sacrifices and offerings for forty years in the desert, O house of Israel? Not at all! You took along the tent of Moloch and the star of the god Rephan, the images you had made for

your cult. For that I will exile you beyond Babylon."

It is human nature to tend to worship things and to invent excuses to keep from meeting the Divine Person, Jesus. Why? Is it because He probes and knows the secrets of our hearts? Isn't this why we shy away from the Word of God? Saint Paul understood this when he spoke to the Hebrews:

Indeed, God's word is living and effective, sharper than any two-edged sword. It penetrates and divides soul and spirit, joints and marrow; it judges the reflections and thoughts of the heart. Nothing is concealed from him; all lies bare and exposed to the eyes of him to whom we must render an account. (Heb. 4:12-13)

In every sacrament, there must be a personal meeting with Jesus. We cannot avoid this meeting. We cannot accept only that part of Him and His Word that suits us and our style of living. Jesus told the Pharisees and scribes at one point:

This means that for the sake of your tradition you have nullified God's word. You hypocrites! How accurately did Isaiah prophesy about you when he said, "This people pays me lip service, but their heart is far from me. They do me empty reverence, making dogmas out of human precepts. (Matt. 15:6-9)

Jesus was speaking to them in regard to the Ten Commandments. Can we not hear Jesus making a similar statement today to our modern churches, which are more concerned about administering the sacraments than in leading their parishioners, through them, into a deep personal and spiritual relationship with Jesus? If we have an awareness of God's love, shouldn't we rely wholeheartedly, trust implicitly, and confide in Jesus for all our needs instead of relying on man and his methods?

Today, thank God, the Church is moving toward a parental role in teaching children individually to have a personal love for Jesus before receiving Jesus in the Sacrament of the Holy Eucharist or the Sacrament of Penance. Jesus never meant that children should be regimented in classes or in large groups like flocks of sheep. When Jesus was on earth, He healed people individually. He loves each one of us as individuals.

David du Plessis, in his book, *The Spirit Bade Me Go* (Logos), points out that we do not become followers of Christ by being born into a particular church or denomination, but only through personal conversion. He writes:

> John the Baptist preached, "Repent you, for the kingdom of heaven is at hand." Jesus preached, "Repent you, for the kingdom of heaven is at hand." On the day of Pentecost, Peter preached,

"Repent . . . and you shall receive the gift of the Holy Ghost. For the promise is unto you, and to your children, and to all that are afar off, even as many as the Lord our God shall call." In the house of Cornelius, Peter told the Gentiles: "Whosoever believeth in Him shall receive remission of sins." Thus it was clear that every Jew and Gentile who came into the Christian church did so by repentance, or conversion, or being born of the Spirit. Every one had a very definite encounter with the Living Christ, the resurrected Son of God. (p. 65)

I have counseled many people, including Catholics, who were only born into their denomination and later found themselves in delinquent or detention homes or penal institutions. They never repented or experienced a conversion, but, ironically, they received the sacraments—without a personal encounter with the *Living Christ.* They never received Jesus into their hearts. Neither did they relinquish their self-will that He might come in and rule their lives through the Holy Spirit.

How different are those whose lives are ruled by God. An outstanding example among my acquaintances was Tom Sullivan who asked the prayer group I was attending to pray after he had been led of the Lord to provide a Christmas dinner for the poor. We prayed, and his direction from Jesus was, *Just follow directions. This is My party.* We continued to pray each day concerning the dinner, and everything began to take shape. There were such surprises as the offer of the use of the Civic Auditorium, food promised from many quarters unknown to us, and work committees organized from volunteers. Newspapers and radio stations publicized the affair, and municipal buses carried free those coming to the dinner. Many bus drivers donated their time on a holiday. The desserts were donated by our parish. Everyone who came was fed, and there was an abundance for all.

In the midst of abundant answers to prayer, the well-received Scripture courses, and my visiting the rest homes in the area, I sensed that my Superior was not pleased with how things were going. One day I received a note from her forbidding me to continue the Scripture courses I had started in the convent. This was distressing news, because I loved conducting those courses. "Not my will but thine be done," I prayed, and continued with my one remaining apostolate of regular visitation at the rest homes.

Not long afterward, a Sister at a nearby convent phoned one day and invited me to attend a retreat given by a visiting priest from New York.

There I met Father Michael Vander Peet, a Sacred Heart priest, who had been baptized in the Holy Spirit and was living at the time in a House of Prayer in Beacon, New York. We had a lengthy conversation on the Holy Spirit, and as I was preparing to leave, he invited me to come east and visit the House of Prayer.

"Why, Father," I exclaimed, "I've never been out of California. But I will keep it in mind. I don't know what Jesus has planned for me." New York seemed so far away, clear across the country, and I put the thought from my mind.

So many people's lives were crossing my path and re-crossing that I no longer was surprised by any sudden development. At the Kathryn Kuhlman service in Los Angeles, I had met a couple from Monterey with a baby they hoped would be cured of a physical ailment. But it didn't happen. At one of my prayer meetings, I met some people who knew relatives of the couple, and they told me how disappointed they were that the baby had not been healed.

I had been reading *The Healing Light* (Logos) by Agnes Sanford, and was intrigued by her explanation that if one parent is Christian, healing could be accomplished at a distance. I telephoned the mother and asked her to hold her baby at approximately three o'clock on Sunday afternoon when two charismatic families and I would be praying for the baby's healing.

That Sunday, we held a small child in proxy for the Monterey child. Later, the mother told us that her child stopped being restless and fell asleep at exactly the time we were praying. For a while, the symptoms of the youngster's disease persisted, but later that week, the child's physician was overwhelmed when tests showed the child to be well.

A short time after this experience, I began to feel that I was not accomplishing what Jesus had planned for me. I did not want for anything physically or materially. I had my health, and my Community provided me with everything necessary for my livelihood. But I felt a lull in my spiritual growth, and I knew I was on dangerous ground, because one does not stand still long. It is a law of spiritual life that we either progress or we retrogress. One evening I spoke to the curate about it.

"Sister, I know how you feel," he said. "Do not be anxious. Jesus knows how you feel, also. Just leave everything to Him, and He will arrange the future for you."

The curate's words brought me a sudden peace within—with no warning that before the week was out, that peace would be shattered.

Chapter 9
And Then, Sudden Changes

Less than a week after the curate told me in so many words to wait upon the Lord, a Sister from a nearby convent telephoned to ask me if I would be interested in a job. Supposing she needed someone to help her, I replied, "Why, yes, if it's something in which I can be of assistance."

"You like to teach Scripture, don't you?" she asked. "And you've had the Pentecostal experience?"

"Yes, Sister. Yes! But—but—what is it you want?"

She said she couldn't tell me over the telephone but would like to see me as soon as possible. When the Sister arrived that afternoon, she explained that someone in New Haven, Connecticut, wanted a Spirit-filled Sister to teach Scripture in the Renewal Center in that city.

Somehow I knew this was an invitation from Jesus—an invitation to step out in faith and rely on Him even more fully than I had in the past. It was His answer to my spiritual problems.

"I'll go! Yes! I'll accept," I told the Sister, and immediately, a quiet, interior peace came over me.

Within a few days, I received a telephone call from the Directress of the Renewal Center. We agreed upon my duties as a teacher of Scripture classes and as a member of the Center. She concluded our conversation with an assurance that I would receive a contractual agreement which I should show to the Mother General to assure her that all was in good order. The papers arrived in due time, and the Mother General examined them.

"What do you wish to do?" she asked.

"I would like a leave of absence to allow me to go to the Renewal Center on a trial basis," I answered.

The Mother General objected, saying the distance was too great and the contract guaranteed no actual security. I then asked if an ex-claustration might be arranged. That, too, was refused.

"Well," I said, "it looks as if I will have to ask for a dispensation from the Community." I had no doubts whatsoever. I knew I was taking the right course. I had known from the time I made my vows that they were made to Jesus and were never altered. He was the One who drew me, invited me to come to Him, encouraged me and preserved me all these years through joys and sorrows, through the good and bad times. He was always there even when I did not actually feel His presence. I had prayed about this new venture and knew He would be with me in the future. There was only one way now open to me, and I knew that way meant stepping out in faith and trusting Jesus *all* the way. John 14:27 came to mind:

> My peace is my gift to you; I do not give it to you as the world gives peace. Do not be distressed or fearful.

While attending a prayer meeting one evening, Rita May, a woman who was visiting friends in the parish and also driving me to rest homes for my visitations, asked for prayer that God might reveal His will to her. After the group disbanded, Tom Sullivan and I prayed together over her. That very night the Lord made it clear to her that she was to return to Flint, Michigan, where she was a member of the Legion of Mary, and take me with her. That same night, the Lord revealed to me that I was going east with Rita. We were surprised and overjoyed the next day, comparing stories, to learn how the Lord had directed each of us.

I wrote an explanatory letter to each of the Superiors in the various convents of my Order, explaining the circumstances involved in my new move, relating that Jesus had invited me to my present Community and now was inviting me to a new life. The Lord gave me a Scripture verse to include in the letters, John 10:27:

My sheep hear my voice. I know them, and they follow me.

I had every intention of continuing as a Sister, so I was permitted to take with me my religious habit, prayer books, and other necessary items, including my charismatic religious books. The dispensation papers arrived from Rome on Valentine's Day, and I was free to go my way to the new life into which Jesus had called me. The Sunday evening before our departure, Rita received the Baptism in the Holy Spirit, and my Community gave me a parting gift of five-hundred dollars. So it was that Rita and I, full and vibrant Christians, drove eastward in her car. We were in God's hands and relied fully upon Him, knowing He would fulfill the promises in Psalm 139:1-10:

O Lord, you have probed me and you know me; you know when I sit and when I stand; you understand my thoughts from afar. My journeys and my rest you scrutinize, with all my ways you are familiar. Even before a word is on my tongue, behold, O LORD, you know the whole of it. Behind me and before, you hem me in and rest your hand upon me. Such knowledge is too wonderful for me; too lofty for me to attain. Where can I go from your spirit? From your presence where can I flee? If I go to the heavens, you are there; if I sink to the nether world, you are present there. If I take the wings of the dawn, if I settle at the farthest limits of the sea, Even there your hand shall guide me, and your right hand hold me fast.

God was my guide and only companion after I left Rita in Flint and took a plane to the Renewal Center in New Haven, Connecticut. The Directress greeted me upon my arrival, and I began attending an exuberant and joyful round of weekend charismatic retreats. I immediately wrote Father Michael Vander Peet, the Spirit-filled Catholic priest whom I had met in California, informing him that I was now settled in the Renewal Center in New Haven and could accept his invitation to visit the House of Prayer in Beacon, New York. It was fortunate for me that I made the contact as soon as I did, because distressing things began to happen in my new home.

I was told one day that I should not make the sign of the cross or wear an exposed cross around my neck, because the Renewal Center was an ecumenical one. I could not hold back a smile the following evening when an Episcopalian gentleman began grace at the table with the sign of the cross.

Next, I was told that this part of the country still had some puritanical hangups, and therefore, it would be better if I would not be so joyful. The "do nots" bothered me, but there were happy times too.

We enjoyed a real Seder meal at the Center before we attended Holy Thursday services at St. Thomas More Chapel. On Good Friday, I participated in the contemporary Stations of the Cross, a reverent act of devotion, including a procession through the city square with a pause for prayers, hymns, Scripture reading, and talks about the responsibility of government.

I was not currently a member of any group of Sisters, so it was suggested that I consider a new Community called Sisters for Christian Community, SFCC, a free form of Christ-committed women. The Community was initiated in 1970 specifically, though not exclusively, as an immediate realization of a collegial Community for Catholic Sisters who do not find it within their conscience to continue to seek religious community within a religious bureaucracy. The members—widows and single women—share the conviction that vocation is not a work but a way of life—a witness to the community nature of the Trinity and of the Church. This uniquely styled Sisterhood is trailblazing a wholly new pattern of living which the members are convinced is needed today for the Church. It has welcomed among its more than three hundred members several Anglican and Byzantine Rite Sisters.

Satisfied with the aims of the Sisters for Christian Community, I wrote to the headquarters in Portland, Oregon, expressing my desire to join, and explaining my background in a traditional congregation. Sister Lillanna Kopp, publisher of the monthly *All-To-All Notes* for the Sisterhood, answered my letter stating that I qualified and would automatically be a member if I chose to be. I chose to be.

A month passed at the Renewal Center, and I still was not teaching Scripture courses. The Directress busied herself with the conditions of the poor and racial problems in the area. My main duties were arranging for the hospitality of weekend guests, a chore I accepted with grace and thankfulness to the Lord. However, I sensed the Directress was not fully satisfied with my efforts. Then one evening she stunned me with the announcement that it would be best for all concerned if I left the Center.

"Oh, God, where do You want me to go?" I asked in prayer, willing to do His bidding.

The answer to my plea came almost immediately in a letter from Father Michael Vander Peet, stating that he was happy that I was settled in the east and would like to have me visit the House of Prayer in Beacon. I had been at the Renewal Center for only six weeks when I found myself packing again for a new destination.

The House of Prayer was housed in the former administration building of a Community of Sisters that had moved to another locality. The elegant English-style three-story structure transferred me to another world, so vast was the acreage of fields, trees, trails, ponds, and creeks. Another Sister and I shared quarters on the top or dormitory floor, which we had to ourselves.

When Father Vander Peet returned from a retreat the day after my arrival, I told him of my new circumstances, and he said, "I will pray about it."

I made new friends—Michaele and Ken Goodman, a couple who had come for a rest after moving from one House of Prayer in New Jersey to another town, and a young man named Bruce, who arrived from Teen Challenge in Brooklyn for a time of prayer, rest, and relaxation. I had heard much about Teen Challenge and Dave Wilkerson, who founded this tremendous work with drug addicts and gang members. Bruce invited me to visit. "Just telephone," he said, "and we can arrange a day." I put the invitation in the back of my mind and forgot about it.

Time was passing, and I still had no definite plans for the future. I did not want to seem impatient, but I did wish the Lord would give me some indication as to His future plans for me. I prayed, "Oh, Lord, where do You want me to be? Do You want me to return to New Haven?"

No! Don't go back. Go ahead, came the reply.

But where? The answer seemed to come in the person of a Sister who suggested that I visit the House of Prayer Experience (HOPE) at Convent Station in New Jersey. Providentially, Michaele and Ken Goodman offered to drive me to Hoboken, where I could board a train for Convent Station. This was really living day by day, with the Lord leading the way.

I thoroughly enjoyed the scenic drive along the Hudson, hardly believing I was looking out on the river I had heard so much about. But nothing surpassed my excitement and surprise when I first caught a glimpse of the New York skyline. Through some misunderstanding, I left the train at Morristown instead of Convent Station and was stranded until a kind gentleman put my belongings in his car and drove me to the front door of Xavier Center on the grounds of St. Elizabeth College at Convent Station.

Here again was a joyful and spiritually uplifting time with charismatic Catholics. Here, too, I received a peek into my future through a prophecy: *You will be going to the afflicted, and oppressed; you will serve the poor with all My love.* Again I had to ask, "But where, oh Lord. Where?"

One day Father Ferry called me into his office. He expressed his concern about my future, and asked where I would be going from there. Honestly, I didn't know, and I told him so. "But don't worry, Father, I added, "Jesus will take care of me. He will find a place for me before I leave here."

I knew in my heart that I still was groping, hoping the Lord would soon show me the way. The world would have called me a fool. But I had confidence in my Lord and knew His ways are not our ways, and that He is never hurried. My search was not to find a place to live and settle down, but to learn God's will.

I recalled that some of the Sisters for Christian Community were living in New Jersey and learned that one of them, Dorothy McSweeney, who taught retarded children, lived close by in Morris Plains. I telephoned her, told her my predicament, and she invited me to come and stay with her until I had definite plans for the future. My heart sang out, "I will give thanks to you, O LORD, with all my heart; I will declare all your wondrous deeds. I will be glad and exult in you; I will sing praise to your name, Most High" (Ps. 9:1-3).

Dorothy called for me the next day, and the drive to her charming cottage was a short but scenic one. The following Sunday afternoon, we were driving home from a picnic when Dorothy decided to call on the wife of an Episcopal rector with whom she had worked. During our conversation, we discussed the charismatic renewal movement in the Catholic Church.

A few days later, I received a phone call from a Spirit-filled Christian, George Wells. He told me that Jesus surprised him one day as he was praying and driving his car in the country. With an outburst of joy and peace which only Jesus can give, he had begun praising God in a beautiful unknown tongue. Alleluia! Our dear Lord is not a formal Master who must have ceremonies and rituals in order to bestow His love and gifts upon us.

George offered to take me to an interdenominational charismatic prayer meeting in Morristown, sponsored by some members of the Full Gospel Business Men's Fellowship, International, and held in a home called the White House, which had a minister in residence. Members of the group conducted Bible studies, held youth meetings, and witnessed in the streets and parks to those needing salvation and seeking rescue from drugs and other addictions.

During the prayer meeting, I was asked to give my testimony. Feeling perfectly at home in an interdenominational group, I told of my personal relationship with Jesus Christ, my healings and Pentecostal experiences. I asked prayers for the Sisters and priests in traditional orders, realizing that many are bound by so much legalism and ritualism that the person of Jesus, His teachings and way of life, remain in the background.

Regardless of what Christian group we are in, no one person has a monopoly on the Holy Spirit. A community cannot maintain a pyramid structure of authority when Jesus bestows His graces and gifts on all— not just on those who are elected or appointed to offices of authority. The early church offers a good example. Saint Peter might have been the spokesman or visible head of the Church, but he did not stop the workings of the Holy Spirit in the life of Saint Paul. Each was given a task and was not to be crushed by those who did not want to take risks in spreading and building up the Christian community. I have met many in authority in religious communities or in parishes where the works of God have not progressed or were even crushed by the narrow-mindedness of box-typed mentality enforced upon parish members and co-workers alike.

After I had given my testimony, a man called Chris handed me some money which I did not wish to accept. "I'm sorry, Sister," he insisted, "but Jesus told me to give this to you." I could not refuse then. Later I discovered that he had handed me a hundred dollars.

Remembering the prophecy given me at HOPE that I was to work with the oppressed and the poor, I decided it would be advantageous for me to visit some of the places having that kind of ministry. God might then lead me further. Embarking on my first visit to New York City, I started out to visit Bruce at Teen Challenge. At the World Trade Center, I asked a policeman, "How do I get to Teen Challenge in Brooklyn?"

He looked at me and replied, in a concerned tone, "You're going to a very bad part of Brooklyn."

"Yes," I replied, "I know. But I'm still going."

After meeting my friend Bruce at Teen Challenge, I suddenly realized that I had gone through Manhattan and on to Brooklyn without being choked by the towering skyscrapers. What miracles Jesus performs!

Bruce gave me a tour of Teen Challenge, including the bookstore. There was supper in the cafeteria around five, and a little later a group of us drove to a small coffeehouse in lower Manhattan called the Living Room. After preparing light refreshments to be served later, we prayed for the power of Jesus and the Holy Spirit to guide and convert those who came through the doors when they opened at eight. At first, people filtered in slowly, but soon the room was crowded. Some came for food, others for companionship. Whenever possible, the conversation was guided to Jesus and His great love for us.

The evening was drawing to a close when a jealous feud exploded between Diane and Willis, regular visitors to the Living Room. Lamps flew through the air, chairs were overturned, and switchblades unsheathed. Of course, we of the Teen Challenge group were praying and binding the evil spirits in Jesus' name. Soon the police arrived, restored order, and peace and calm returned—

but not for long.

Diane thought our group had called the police. She went to a parked car belonging to a Teen Challenge couple and yanked out some wires. As it turned out, she had pulled wires connected to the windshield wipers, so no real damage was done. At 3:00 A.M., we drove back to Brooklyn without further mishap.

One Wednesday evening, Bruce took me to an inspiring prayer meeting held at Fordham University in the lower hall of St. Thomas More Chapel. It included a "Life in the Spirit" seminar, a prayer time, Mass, and then a discussion of some spiritual insights of the charismatic movement. Attendance was predominantly Catholic, although other denominations were represented.

Next, I visited Dorothy Day's Soup Kitchen at the St. Joseph's House of Hospitality on Skid Row in the Bowery. What I saw there was heartrending—I knew it was God's work. But was it His work for me?

I was seeing much of New York City, but still had no concrete leading from the Lord as to what He would have me do. As a climax to my week in the great metropolis, I visited some Sisters for Christian Community. We opened our Bibles and read whatever Scripture was before us. Then, as each Sister shared the spiritual insight she received, a theme or subject developed, giving enlightenment and encouragement to us all.

During the week, at my Bible reading periods, I opened the Book five times to Acts 18:8-11, and each time I read, I received a clearer picture of where Jesus wanted me to work:

> Many of the Corinthians, too, who heard Paul believed and were baptized. One night in a vision the Lord said to Paul: "Do not be afraid. Go on speaking and do not be silenced, for I am with you. No one will attack you

or harm you. There are many of my people in this city." Paul ended by settling there for a year and a half, teaching them the word of God.

God was telling me this was where I belonged, in New York City, working with the poor and the oppressed. But something in me was still rebellious, procrastinating.

For many years, I had wanted to see Baroness Catherine de Hueck and Father Eddie Dougherty's Madonna House in Ontario, Canada, a training center for Lay Apostolates, and so I wrote a letter asking the Baroness if I might visit their well-known center for a few weeks after attending the Charismatic Conference at Notre Dame University. Her quick, cordial reply assured me of a warm welcome.

Before leaving for Notre Dame, I heard the Lord speak to my inner being in an authoritative manner as I lay in bed. *I want you, Sister,* He seemed to say, *to work in the Soup Kitchen in New York City.*

Although that was what I wanted to do, my human weakness came forth, and I responded, "But Lord, I have never worked among those kinds of people." I thought of the ragged, dirty derelicts I had seen on my visit there.

The next words brought tears to my eyes. *Sister, I died for each man you are going to serve. I love each and every one of them.*

I have often wondered why Jesus had such patience with me for surely my reply this time must have tried Him. "But Lord," I remonstrated, "I have only nice dresses. How can I work down there?"

Back came the decisive but Fatherly reply: *Buy some smocks, Sister, and get to work.*

Despite this inner conversation with Jesus, the prophecy and the words from Scripture directing me to work among the poor and the derelicts, I still had to put out my fleece, to be absolutely sure it was God's will.

"Lord," I said, "if all this points to where You want me to do Your work, I would like a Catholic priest to verify it; to tell me it is God's will."

God has unusual ways to work out His will as I soon would learn.

Chapter 10
End of the Search

"God is never in a hurry but He is always on time."

How many times I had to tell myself that fact to fully impress it upon my mind as I planned to attend the Charismatic Conference at Notre Dame. One well-laid transportation plan after another fell through as the time of the Conference drew nearer and nearer. It seemed that every avenue closed, and then in a prayer meeting at Convent Station, Father Ferry permitted me to announce that I wanted to go to the Notre Dame Conference but had no way of getting there. There was no response.

"Lord, You know best," I said and resigned myself to missing the conference.

While I was walking out of the prayer meeting, a handsome young man came up to me and introduced himself as Jim Delevan, a member of the core group at the Fordham University prayer meetings. He asked if I was the person looking for a ride to Notre Dame. "There is room in my car," he said.

I could have hugged him, but suddenly it occurred to me that I was not wearing my veil. Almost fearfully I asked, "Do you mind that I am a Sister?"

"Great!" he replied. "That will make it all the merrier." Then he explained that he had not planned to attend the prayer meeting. The leading of God had brought him there. "Now I understand," he said.

There were five of us in a compact car, making close spiritual fellowship inevitable as we drove westward from Morris Plains, New Jersey, toward the Conference. We also had our problems. It was night and we had been on the road about five hours when a deer jumped into the road. The car hit him but Jim's expert driving kept the car from overturning. A quick survey showed nothing more serious than a slightly bent front bumper and the glass smashed in one headlight. We all expressed our sorrow over the deer and started on our way again. Almost immediately, the engine became overheated. Here we were in the Allegheny Mountains of Pennsylvania in the middle of the night, with car trouble. We managed to nurse the car to a service station at the next turnpike exit, where we learned that our collision with the deer had caused the radiator to leak. The service station mechanic was unable to repair the damage, but he gave us three big oil containers filled with water.

We had a big laugh each time we

were forced to stop and wait for the radiator to cool, refill it with water, and then drive on. My thoughts returned to Miss Lotta Rattles and her old-age problems. We finally reached a little town with garage facilities, but found it would be necessary for us to spend the remainder of the night at a nearby motel while waiting for the car to be repaired.

God was doing His thing. After a refreshing sleep and good food, we had an enjoyable and cheerful prayer meeting in the motel. We also found some lovely back roads and a picturesque river to walk along. We were drinking in everything God was providing, including spiritual fellowship, in preparation for the Conference. On the road again in the afternoon, we arrived at Notre Dame that evening, missing very little of the Conference.

The Conference offered an unusual inspirational challenge as David du Plessis, Leland Davis, Bishop Joseph

McKinney, and many others ministered to us. I saw Rita May again, and other old friends. My future was so unsettled that I began referring to myself as "the floating nun."

Following the Conference, I took a train to Chicago, a plane to Toronto, and a bus to Combermere, Canada, where I telephoned The Madonna House. A driver called for me and whisked me to a two-story wooden structure where I was ushered upstairs to a women's dormitory. The furnishings were quite frugal, the facilities meager. The country living style was not for novelty or necessity but, rather, for practicing little self-denials and acts of penance that the present-day secular world has long since dropped and forgotten. Intending to stay for two weeks, I hurriedly unpacked and joined others for Vespers in the Chapel.

The Madonna House has been a training center since 1947 for lay members of its apostolate who spend three years in training preparatory to doing missionary work and putting into practice their promises of poverty, chastity, and obedience. There are also summer programs for young adults eighteen to twenty-five years of age, and retreatants (men and women) throughout the year. It is a community of Christian love, with the members striving to live the Gospel without compromise, loving and serving one another.

We all arose at 6:30 a.m. and assembled in the Chapel for Lauds and meditation, followed by Mass at 7:40. Breakfast was served at 8:30. During the morning, I worked on the publication, *Restoration,* with a break for lunch at noon combined with spiritual reading and a discussion. It was extremely uplifting to be with so many lay people who were hungry for the Word of God.

During the afternoon, I had a tour of the grounds and buildings, including the new Eastern Rite Chapel (the rite to which Father Eddie Dougherty belongs), the laundry, kitchen, library, handicraft workshop, gift shop, flea market, and Pioneer Museum.

I planned to celebrate the feast of the Sacred Heart of Jesus by fasting and praying in one of the log houses of prayer located in the fields and forest on the House of Madonna grounds. These prayer houses are equipped with a chair, table, Bible, woodburning stove for winter use, and an oil lamp. A loaf of bread and a thermos of tea or coffee provide the only sustenance for the day or a maximum of three days. When I asked about acquiring one of the houses of prayer, I was told to consult one of the priests. I selected Father Emile Briere, telling him I wished to fast and pray for a special intention. Before I realized what was happening I had recounted my reasons for leaving California, starting a new vocation in the east, and explaining how

Jesus was leading me.

"I think it is God's will that you work in the Soup Kitchen," he said, immediately after I finished my story.

My heart leaped for joy. "Oh, Father!" I exclaimed. "You spoke the words I was waiting to hear. Your words were the outward sign I had asked Jesus to give me as confirmation of His will."

Father Briere nodded. "What you need, Sister, after all this searching, is a good rest before you plunge into your new work," he said. "I suggest you take a month off."

"A rest! A month off!" I exclaimed with delight. "I would like to start right now—but where do you think I should go?"

"Well," Father Briere said, "since the Madonna House is a training center, and you have already had plenty of training, I suggest you stay at the YWCA in Ottawa. I can let one of the girls drive you to the bus station. You can see the city while you rest from your labors."

I thanked Father Briere for his help and packed my bags again.

While I was in Ottawa, I knew God's will, but to transfer it into practical application was something else. I knew no one in New York City with whom I might live even temporarily. One day when I was thinking about the matter, Chris, the man at the White House in Morristown who had given me such a generous contribution, came to my mind. I wrote him, inquiring if any of his acquaintances might know someone in Manhattan who could offer me a temporary residence while I worked in the Soup Kitchen and looked for a job.

A week before I left Canada, I received a letter from Chris, informing me that a nurse in Manhattan, Vreni Huber, might possibly take me in temporarily. I wrote her immediately, and received her gracious, affirmative reply shortly before my departure. God's timetable was operating according to His will.

During the bus ride to New York City, through the beautiful scenic countryside, my heart filled with gratitude for all that God had done for me. I wanted to sing out:

> I will give thanks to you, O LORD, with all my heart, (for you have heard the words of my mouth;) in the presence of the angels I will sing your praise; I will worship at your holy temple and give thanks to Your name, Because of your kindness and your truth; for you have made great above all things your name and your promise. When I called, you answered me; you built up strength within me. (Ps. 138: 1-3)

This was the beginning of a second vocation for me. What did God have planned? My future was still hidden from me, but I had taken out a policy in the King's Insurance Company, and in His complete coverage, I knew He would provide as He had in the past.

Chapter 11
The Overflowing Cup

When I stepped off the bus at the Port Authority, it was after eight o'clock, so I decided to spend the night at an inexpensive Catholic hotel. After I told the desk clerk I would be spending only one night at the hotel because I would be moving in with friends, he graciously offered to drive me and my luggage the next evening to the apartment in upper East Manhattan.

Once ensconced in my hotel room, I telephoned Vreni Huber and asked if I could meet her the next day. She seemed delighted. "I do hope I'm not barging in on you," I said.

"No, Sister," came the reassuring reply. "I'm always having friends in to stay for a while. You are most welcome."

That night at the hotel seemed endless. I tossed and turned, listening to the sounds of screeching brakes, automobile horns, police and fire sirens, and the many other night noises of the great metropolis. I asked myself, "Is this the place I am to live—with all these distractions?" I turned to the Lord and pleaded, "Oh, Lord, You will let me get used to it, won't You?"

The next day, I visited Vreni in her two-bedroom walk-up apartment on the fifth floor in upper East Manhattan, away from the downtown noise and traffic. Late in the afternoon, I returned to the hotel for my luggage. The clerk was there also with his wife and their baby, and he drove me back to my apartment. It wasn't until after

I had thanked him, and his family had gone on their way, that I realized that I would have to carry my two suitcases and a garment bag up five flights of stairs. There was no one in the apartment to help me, so I was my own porter. It wouldn't have been possible for me to do such a thing before my back was healed. Praise the Lord!

I telephoned Dorothy Day to report that I would be in the next morning. After I explained my temporary accommodations, she said, "You probably will find a part-time job soon and may be able to rent one of the apartments across the street." I assured her that the Lord would find me something.

Working on the soup line, I would be free to use the afternoons to seek employment. Some of those helping at St. Joseph's Hospitality House volunteered their services during weekends and worked at secular jobs during the week, but I decided the soup line would be a five-day week for me. I was eager to assist Dorothy Day in any way possible because I had long been impressed with her work.

She and Peter Maurin established the *Catholic Worker* newspaper in 1933 in an effort to bring the Catholic Church into the social action movement spawned by the Depression. I had heard about the paper many times over the years.

I first saw Dorothy when she spoke at the University of Santa Clara before I left California. She impressed me then as a very sincere Christian trying to follow Christ's teachings in the social and economic areas. I saw her later at Sacred Heart University in Bridgeport, Connecticut, where she addressed a group of students, drawing scenes from the Gospels relevant to present-day social problems. I appreciated her efforts to put into practice the social aspects of the Gospels; however, I knew that any social work which remains only on the level of humanitarianism leaves vacant the supernatural enlightenment stemming from love and concern for the individual. Dorothy Day's work left no such vacuum. The soup kitchen was only one example of the depth of her involvement.

One day my attention was especially drawn to a young man who came through the soup line. His face and entire demeanor made me think of a drowned rat. His shoulders were bent, his hair not combed, and his face was stained with grime. One can expect such things in a soup line, but this boy was so young. After lunch, when everyone had finished eating, I asked him, "Is there anything I can do to help you?" That was all he needed.

"Oh, Sister!" he blurted out. "I don't know what to do. My buddy and I went to Los Angeles from St. Louis. Then we saw an advertisement in the paper about a good prospect, a good deal here in New York.

We crossed the country, but when we arrived here, it all fell through. Besides that, my so-called buddy has left me high and dry. He disappeared with all our money. Can you imagine that? I don't know where to go. I haven't a red cent. I don't want to sleep on the streets or in a doorway. I've never done that."

"Have you asked about staying here for the night?" I inquired. "If they have room upstairs on the fourth or fifth floor, I'm sure they will let you bunk for a while. Even if they haven't, ask them if you can sleep on a bench downstairs. It's better than being outside in the streets."

"Do you think they'll let me?" he asked. His whole expression changed.

"Of course they will. And you could help with the dishes now if you like, or with the preparations for supper."

When I returned from a visit to the Catholic Church around the corner, he was a new boy, happily washing dishes. Drying his hands, he came over to me, and said, "Sister, it's all fixed. I can stay until my father sends me money to come home. I wired him and he wired back that everything is all right. Gee, Sister, thanks. I won't try a risky thing like that again."

Later, I received a postcard from the young man, expressing his thanks again. He had a safe trip home, and everything was fine.

At St. Joseph's House of Hospitality, preparation of the special soup for the day begins at seven-thirty in the morning. Bread and butter, donated daily, are placed on the table and replenished many times, together with hot tea in pitchers. Before nine-thirty each morning, a line of men has formed outside. The doors open shortly before ten, and the men are taken to the lower floor where benches are provided for seating them. Serving starts at ten. The number of men served varies between 150 and 250. Many times as I serve the men, I recall the words of Jesus: *I love each one that you will serve. I died for each man.*

I treasure the privilege of working in the soup line. As I look upon the Crucifix on the wall, or the picture of Jesus crowned with thorns, I understand the meaning of true love. True love always entails *sacrifice.*

Most of the staff stays on for supper and evening vespers. Each Monday night there is a Eucharistic banquet, and on Friday evenings, invited outside speakers address a meeting of the workers and homeless men. The talk is followed by an open discussion.

Often someone I am serving will ask, "Why are you people so kind to us?" I answer, "Do you remember the last commandment that Jesus gave His apostles before the Crucifixion? He told them to 'Love one another as I have loved you.' We are loving you."

Many come to the soup kitchen under the influence of liquor and drugs, but Christian love can change a man. And I have seen it happen.

One day I came across Isaiah 58, and it reminded me of the fruitful works of the St. Joseph's House of Hospitality, not only the soup line but the shelter provided for the homeless, and the clothing room across the street where men and women may obtain clothing year-round at no cost. Through the prophet Isaiah, God tells us:

> This, rather, is the fasting that I wish: releasing those bound unjustly, untying the thongs of the yoke; Setting free the oppressed, breaking every yoke; Sharing your bread with the hungry, sheltering the oppressed and the homeless; Clothing the naked when you see them, and not turning your back on your own . . . If you bestow your bread on the

hungry and satisfy the afflicted;
Then light shall rise for you in
the darkness, and the gloom
shall become for you like mid-
day; Then the Lord will guide
you always and give you plenty
even on the parched land. He
will renew your strength, and
you shall be like a watered garden, like a spring whose water
never fails.

(Isa. 58: 6-7, 10-11)

The Lord was blessing me bounti-
fully, but there was more to come, as
I learned on the day I had been at
Vreni's for one week. That day Verna, Vreni's roommate, received a
telephone call asking if she knew of
anyone who could be an overnight
companion for a woman who lived in
New York and was not in the best of
health.

"No, I don't," she told the caller.
"However, my roommate is a nurse.
She might be able to help you. Call
back tomorrow evening. She will be

home then."

Almost before Verna finished with the call, a voice said to me, *That job is for you.*

I spoke to Vreni and Verna about it, and an interview was arranged for me. There would be no domestic work or cooking. Others were engaged for those duties. I would simply act as a companion, available overnight when needed, and I would live in the apartment. Beyond that, my time was my own—I could work in the soup kitchen. I took the assignment as being from the hand of God. All my financial needs were met. He had filled my cup to overflowing.

It would be ten days before I could move in, because some of the apartment was being repainted, so that weekend, I visited Chris and his family in New Jersey, eternally grateful to them for their financial assistance and their bringing me to know Vreni and Verna.

Moving day arrived. I packed my

things and took a taxi to my new address. A canopy, a doorman, an elevator operator—these were luxuries I had not known before. The elevator whizzed me to the twelfth floor, and I entered my new home—a penthouse with maid service, and my dinner served every evening except two. The lovely private room and bath with French windows, a terrace with shrubs, vines, small trees, and larger plants of rhododendron surrounding three sides of the spacious five rooms —I thought I was dreaming.

I could utter with David:

From heaven the LORD looks down; he sees all mankind. From his fixed throne he beholds all who dwell on the earth, he who fashioned the heart of each, he who knows all their works . . . Our soul waits for the LORD, who is our help and our shield, For in him our hearts rejoice; in his holy name we trust. May your kindness, O LORD, be upon us

who have put our hope in you.
(Ps. 33: 13-15; 20-22)

Comfortably situated in New York City, I now had time to follow as the Holy Spirit led.

I attended the prayer meetings at Fordham University several times but I was always so late coming home on the subway that it bothered me. One day, someone mentioned the Full Gospel Business Men's Fellowship International's prayer meetings on Monday evenings in the Americana Hotel. I began attending them, in addition to attending prayer meetings in New Jersey. I had spoken twice in California at breakfasts sponsored by the FGBMFI. It was a joy to again join this great ecumenical fellowship of Spirit-filled people. Through contact with them, I have been privileged to give my testimony on several occasions and find that such testimonies are helpful in removing barriers to Christian unity. With Jesus in the center of our worship, we can be one in heart, mind and spirit. Praise the Lord!

Soon, I felt drawn once again to a Prison and Detention Home Apostolate. I taught for several months at Rikers Island in Queens, New York, and then began teaching a group of women in maximum security at Elmhurst General Hospital. Two Sisters for Christian Community, another zealous Christian contacted through the FGBMFI, and I have worked as a team to bring the Good News to these women prisoners. We find them very receptive.

One day, in the Catholic diocesan paper, I noticed an advertisement for a religious teacher in the Confraternity of Christian Doctrine program. I ignored it for three weeks and then came to grips with what I knew the Lord was asking me to do and volunteered to teach religion in the afternoons to Brother Anthony's Junior High School classes. These Harlem boys responded well to love and concern for them and to the Word of God.

The local Gideons presented each student with a New Testament, and supplied Bibles also for the women prisoners.

Looking back over the work our Lord has led me to do during my stay in New York City, I remembered the prophecy given to me at Shiloh Temple in California:

> "For the name of the Lord in you has been greatly honored, My daughter. And I shall increase your knowledge and your understanding of My divine purposes. Yes, in you there shall be a quickening that you have not known heretofore. And your eyes shall be anointed with eyesalve. And you shall see the beauty of the King of kings. And you shall portray to others, and communicate that which the Lord has birthed in your own spirit. Yes, the Lord has brought

you through a strange path, but He has brought you to this hour that He might lead you into pastures green, that He might lead you into areas you have not known heretofore, and you can believe Him in faith, for He shall surely be with you. Fear you not; He shall surely be with you. He shall not leave you nor forsake you. He shall not cause you to turn aside in any way to pastures that shall not be green, and that shall not be able to be—yes—hearts that shall not receive. For I shall cause people to come, and they will be drawn by your spirit, and you will be able to rightly divide unto them the Word of the Lord."

Praise God, the prophecy has proved true, and with all Christians everywhere, I can confidently sing Isaiah's song of thanksgiving:

God indeed is my savior; I am confident and unafraid. My

strength and my courage is the Lord, and he has been my savior. With joy you will draw water at the fountain of salvation, and say on that day: Give thanks to the Lord, acclaim his name; among the nations make known his deeds, proclaim how exalted is his name. Sing praise to the Lord for his glorious achievement; let this be known throughout all the earth. Shout with exultation, O city of Zion, for great in your midst is the Holy One of Israel! (Isa. 12:2-6)

And, praise God, I can not only sing my thanksgiving—I who once could barely walk have been set free—in my body and in my spirit—to leap for joy! Hallelujah!